Flowers & Flair
Art Coloring Pages
Volume II

By
Kathy Carman Henderson

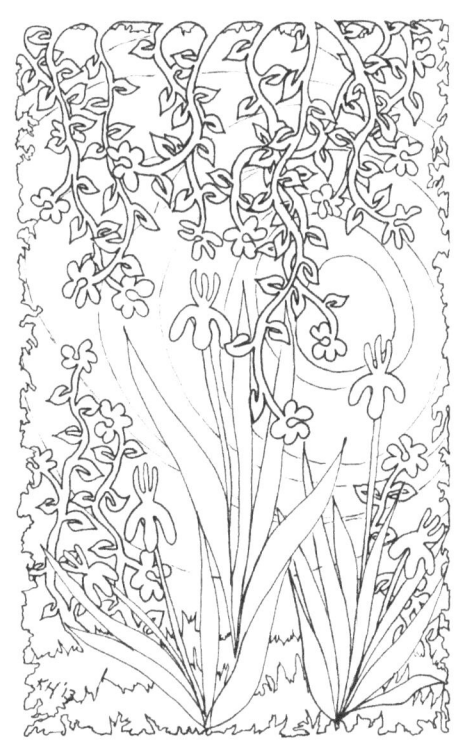

Kathy Carman Henderson

Copyright © 2013 Anna Kathleen (Carman) Henderson
All rights reserved.
ISBN: 1494833255
ISBN-13: 978-1494833251

Dear fellow artist,

    Here is the second volume of my freehand drawings to color. This book has 5 more designs than the first – still with 2 copies of each – so you can try different colors and techniques. I hope you enjoy them!

    I use colored pencils, but feel free to try crayons, watercolors, markers, or any other medium you desire. If you are using a medium requiring firm pressure, you may want to put a piece of cardboard under your drawing, so the surface of the next design isn't damaged. If you use a wet medium, I suggest you tear the page out before starting work.

    I also have a question for you. I am curious as to which designs are most liked or not liked. I am especially interested in comments by people with Autism Spectrum traits. Do my designs bother you or give you enjoyment? If they do bother you, may I suggest creating your own designs with one of several graph paper websites.

    To give me feedback, please do so by rating and commenting on these books on Amazon.

    Have fun and God bless you,
        Kathy Carman Henderson

Kathy Carman Henderson

Flowers & Flair

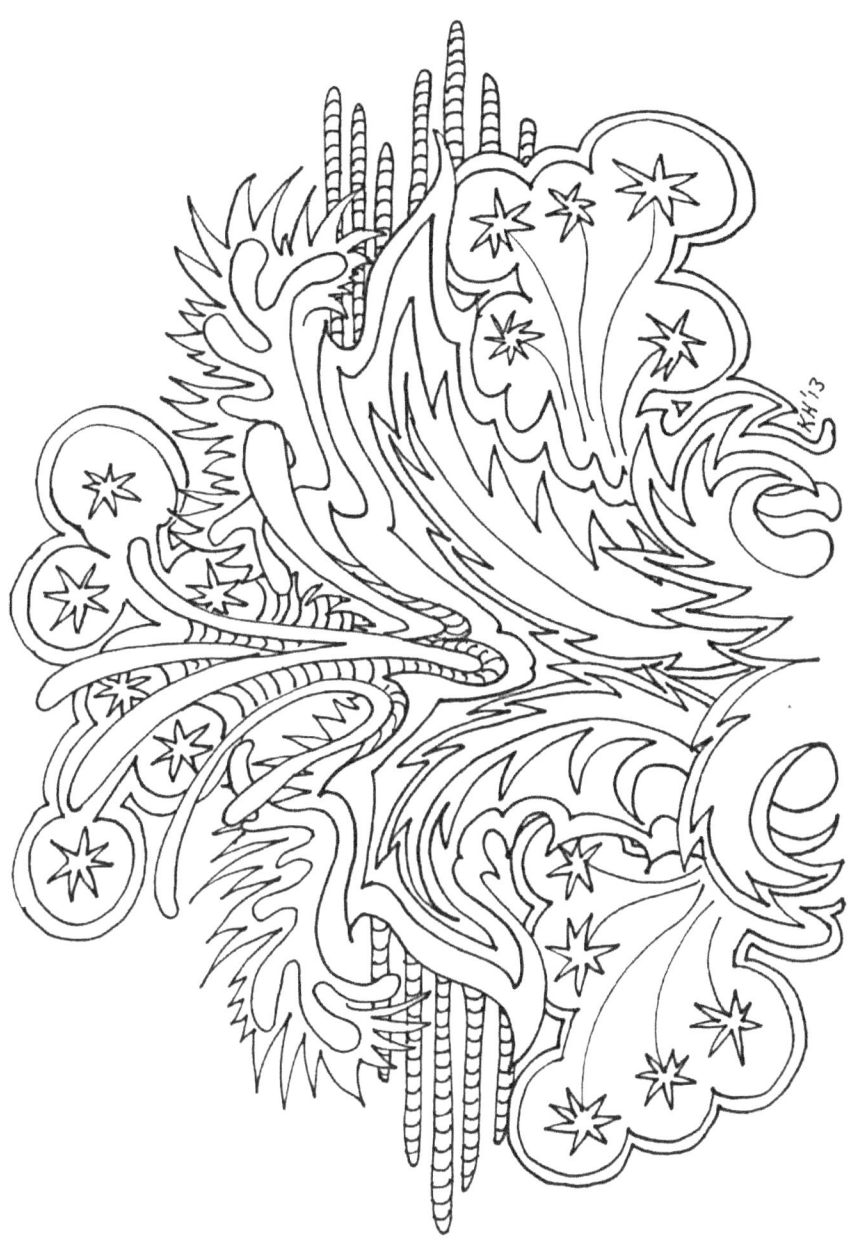

Kathy Carman Henderson

Flowers & Flair

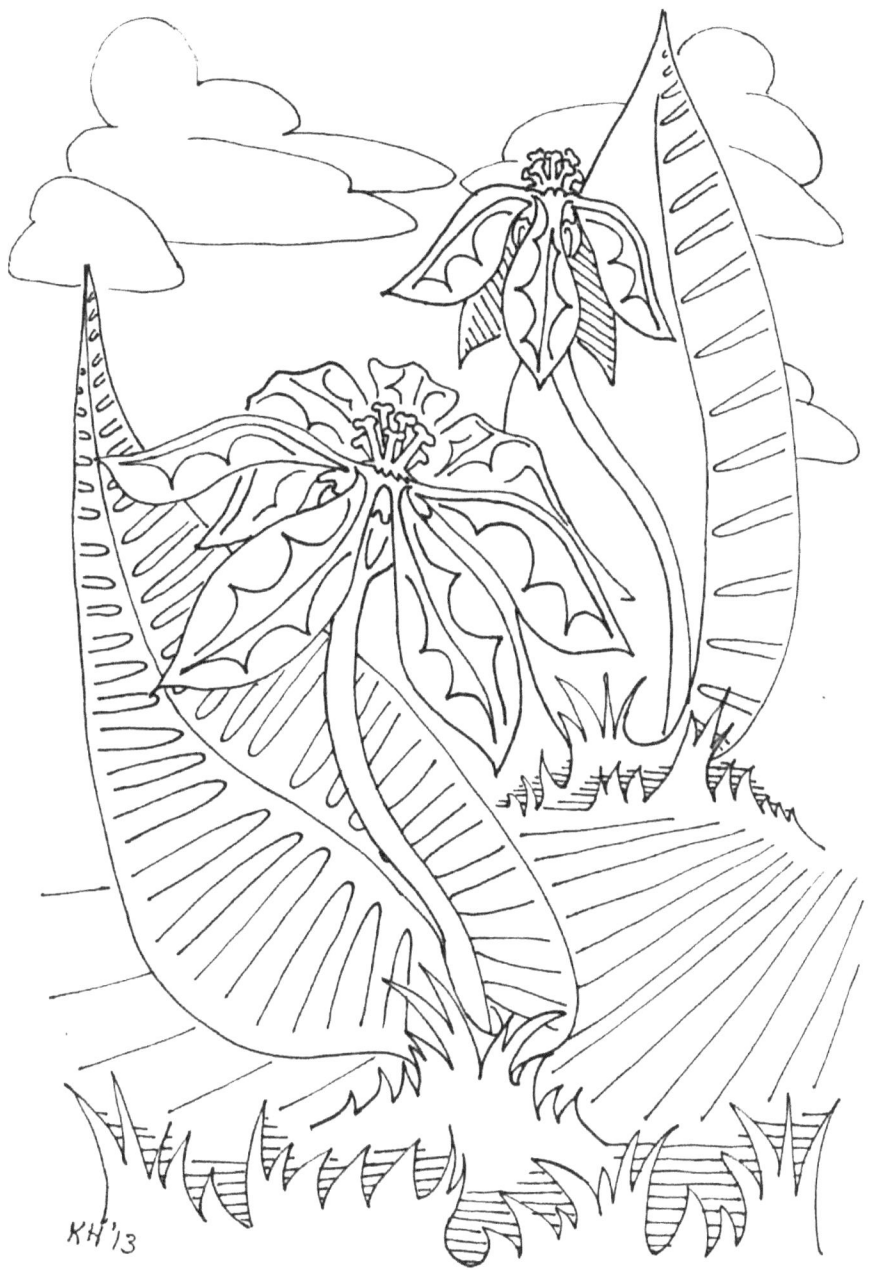

Kathy Carman Henderson

Flowers & Flair

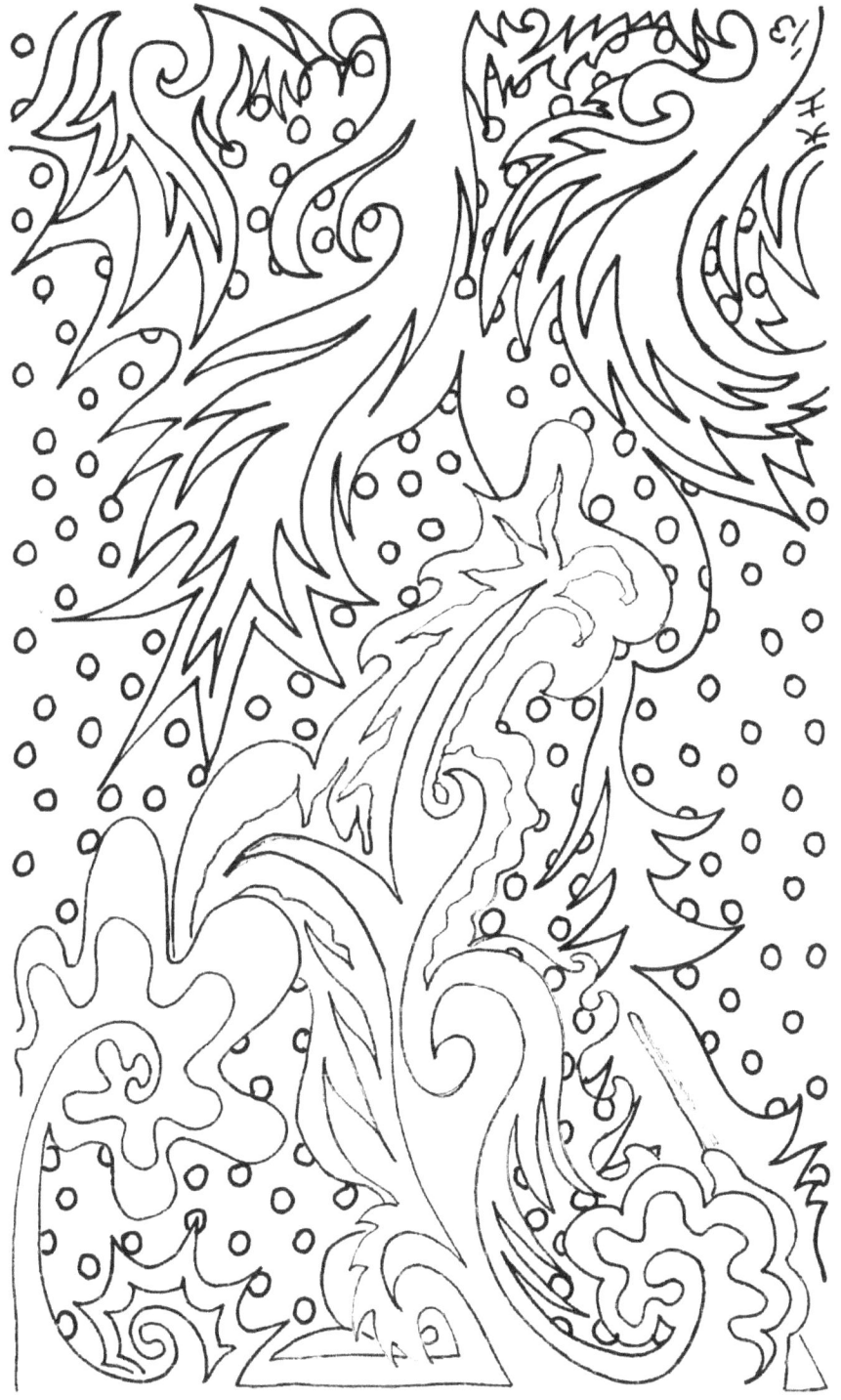

Kathy Carman Henderson

Flowers & Flair

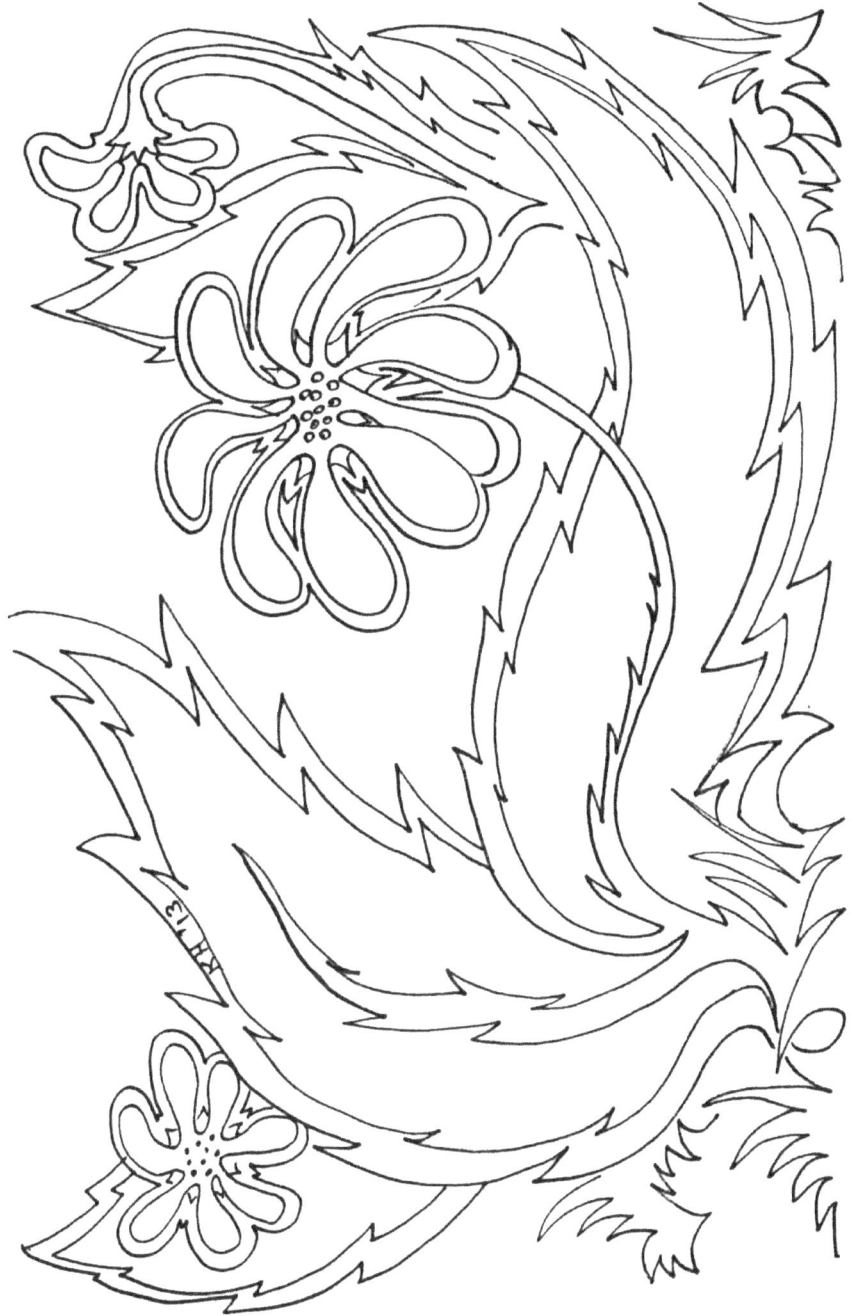

Kathy Carman Henderson

Flowers & Flair

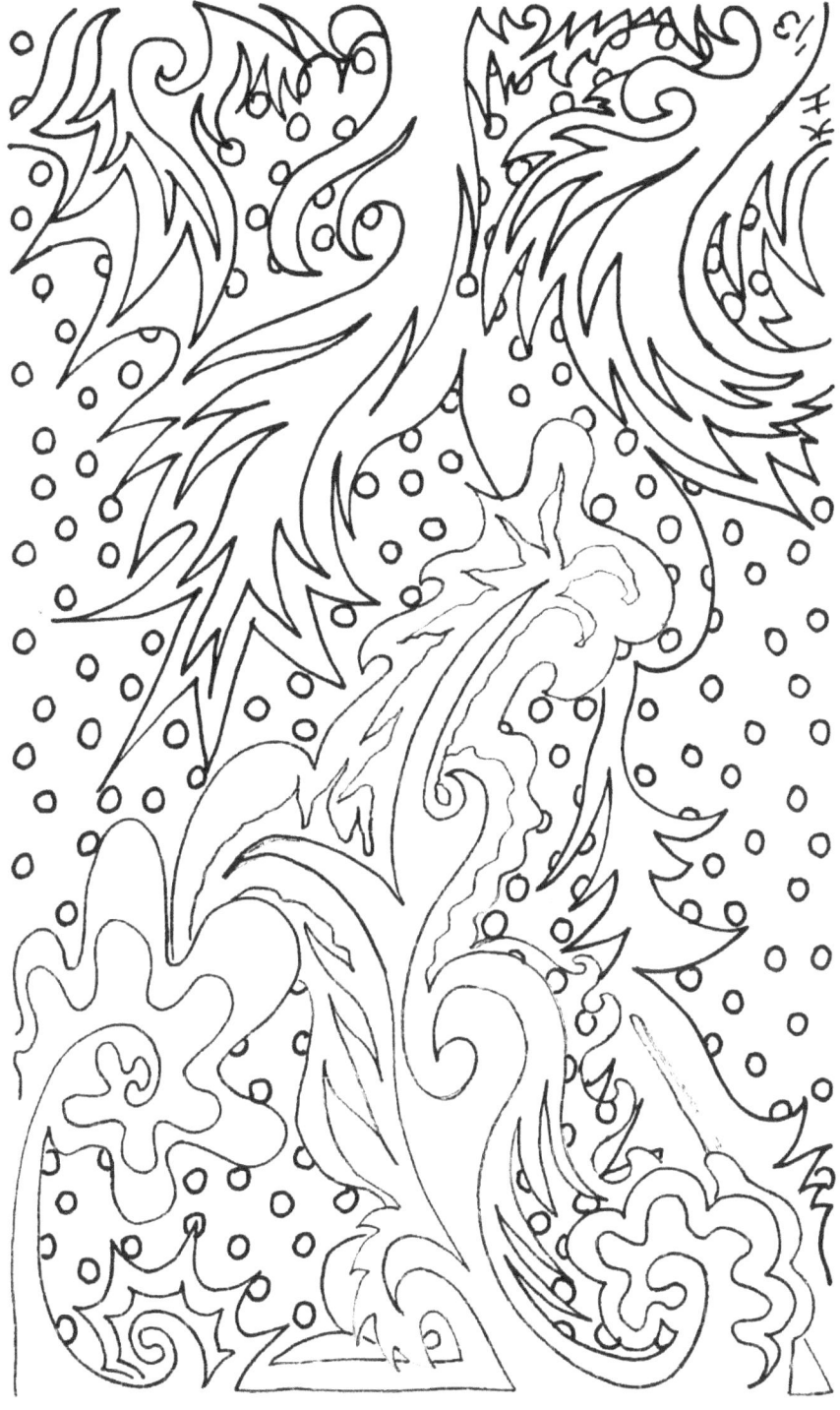

Kathy Carman Henderson

Flowers & Flair

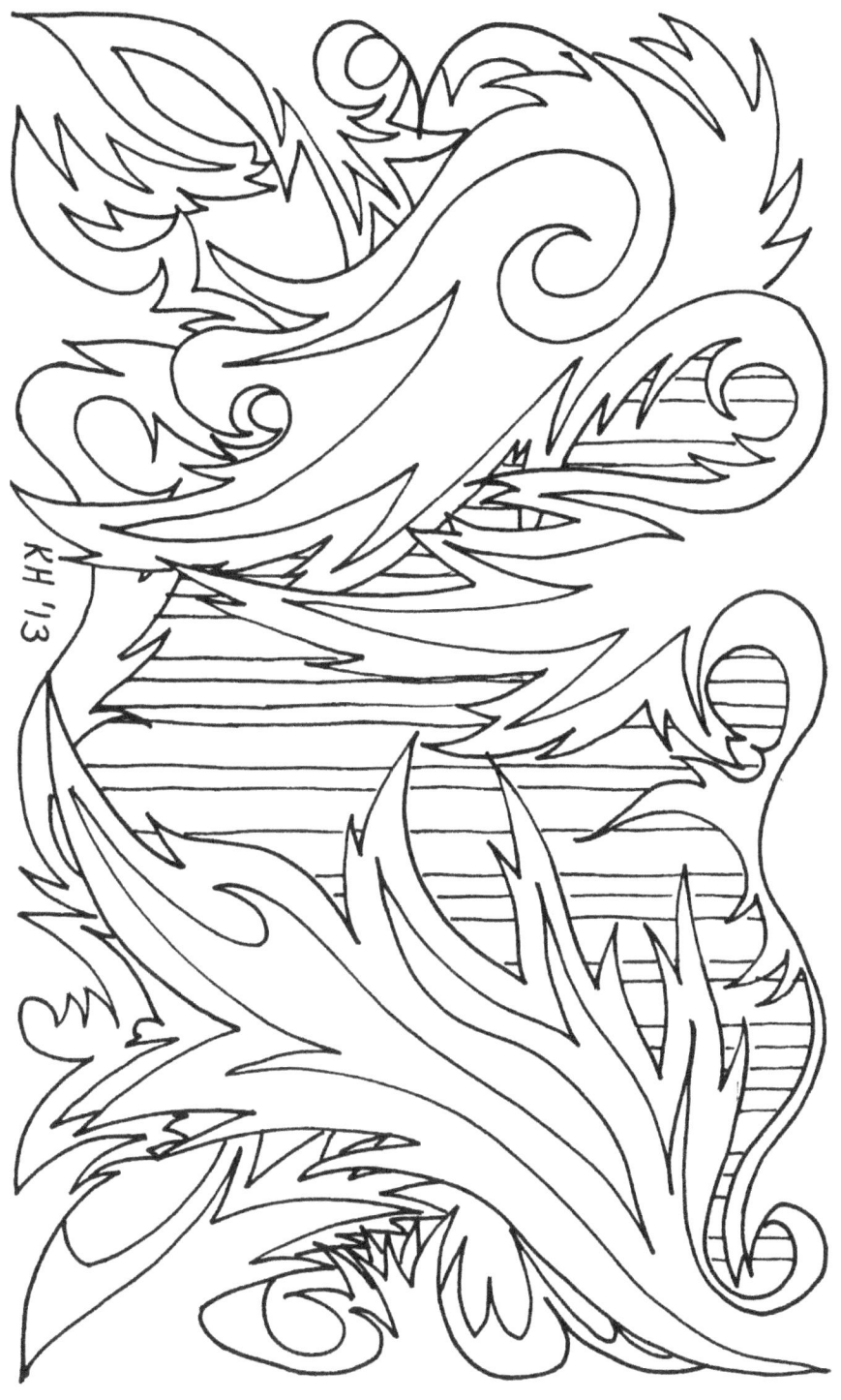

Kathy Carman Henderson

Flowers & Flair

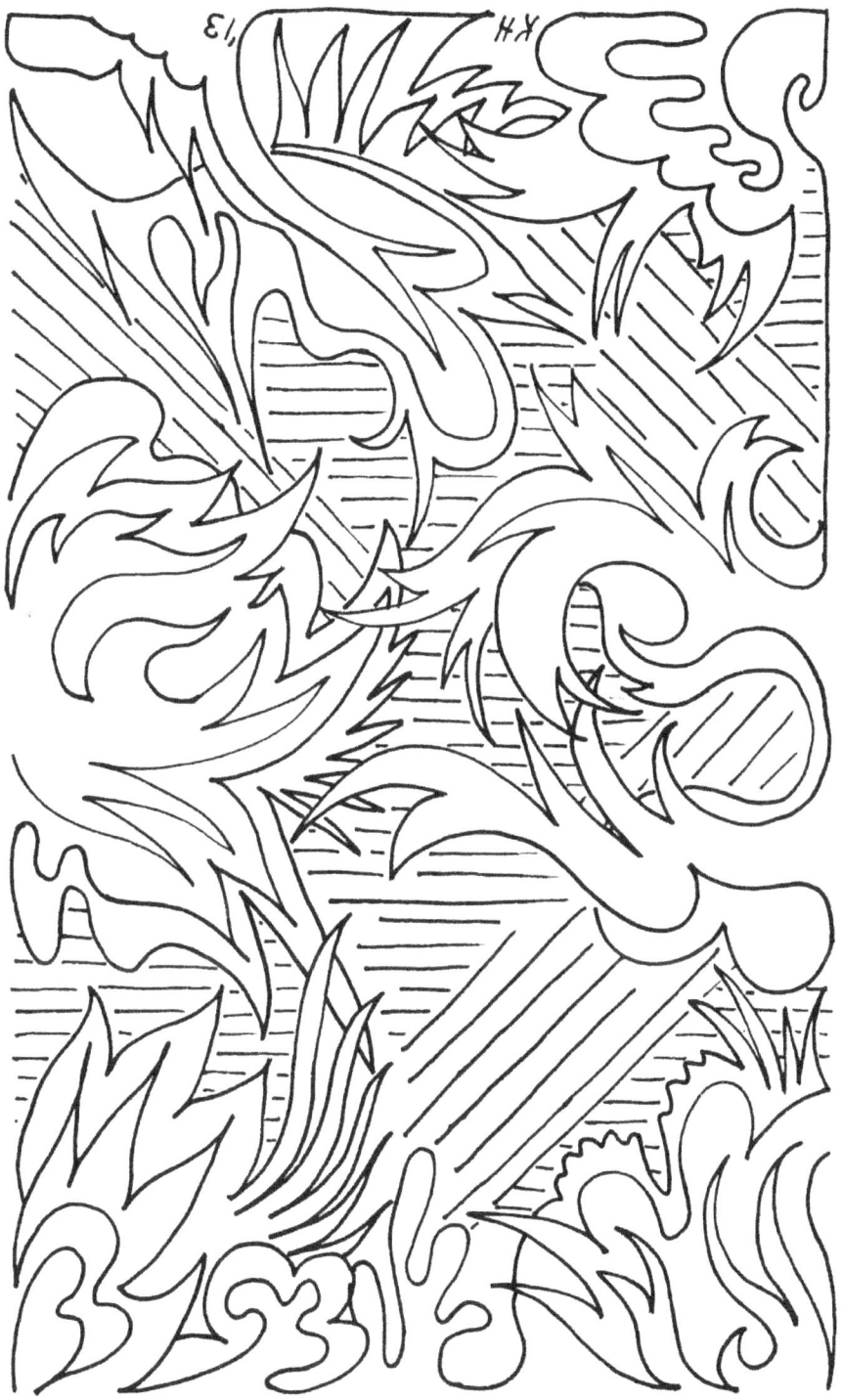

Kathy Carman Henderson

Flowers & Flair

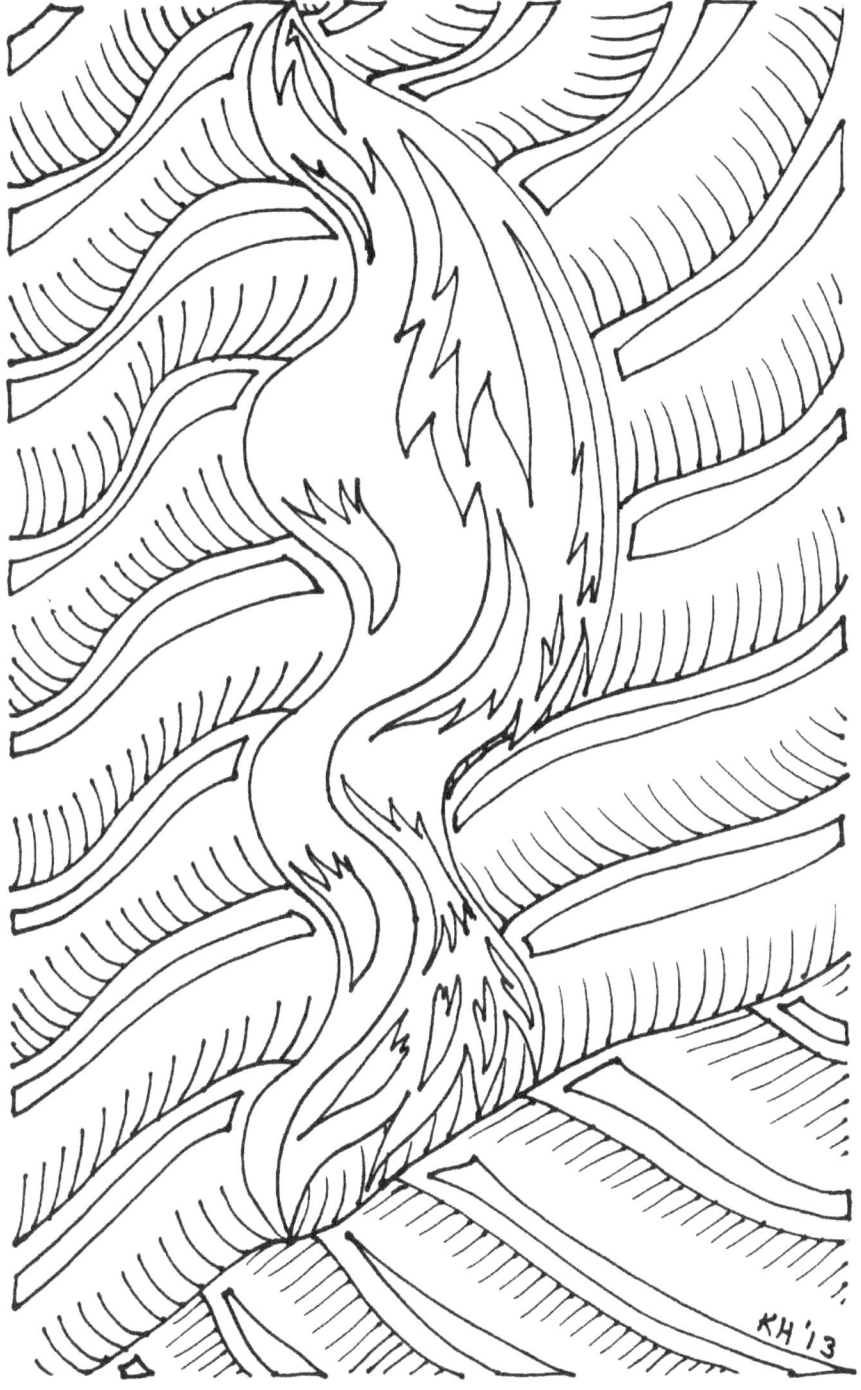

Kathy Carman Henderson

Flowers & Flair

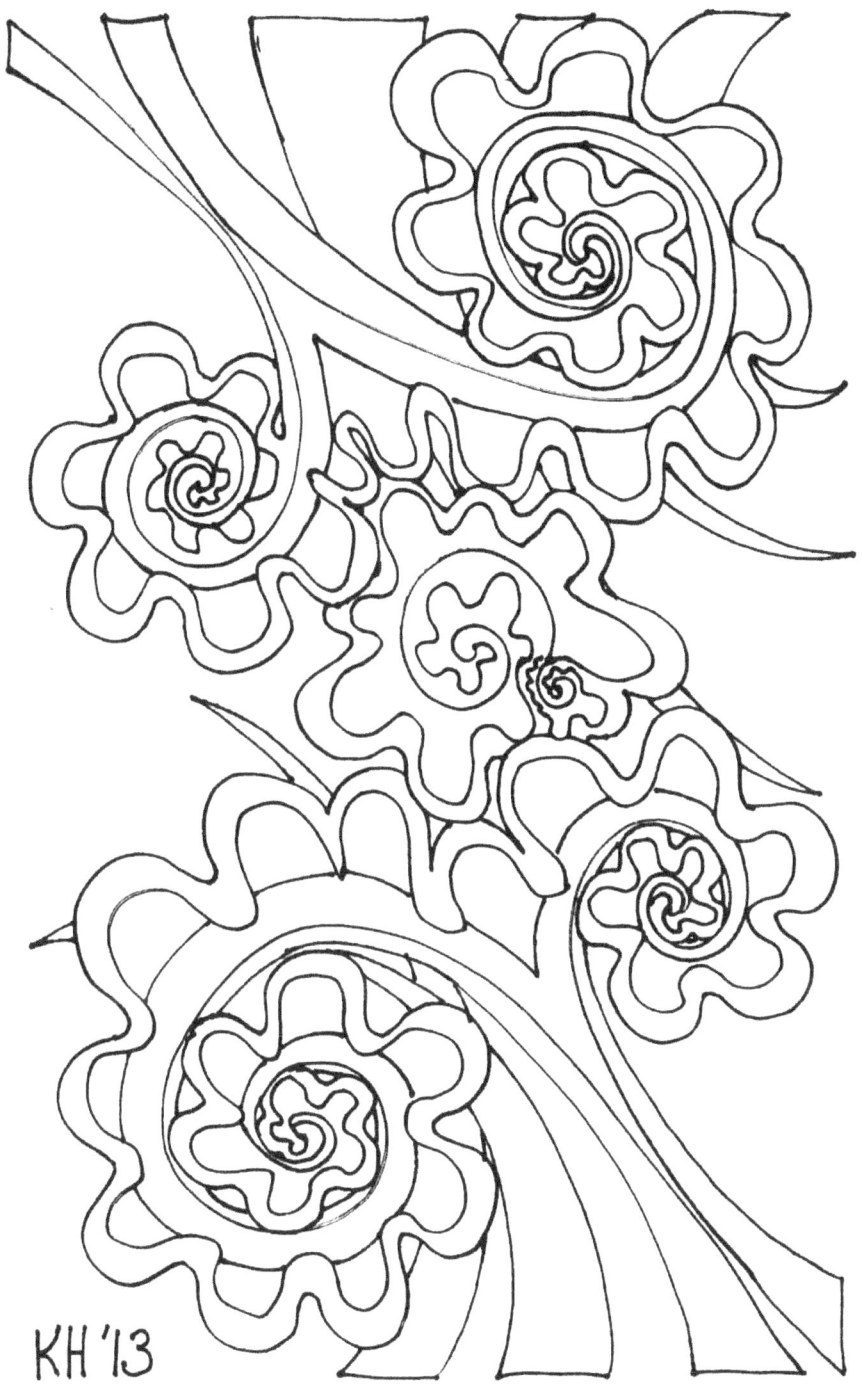

Kathy Carman Henderson

Flowers & Flair

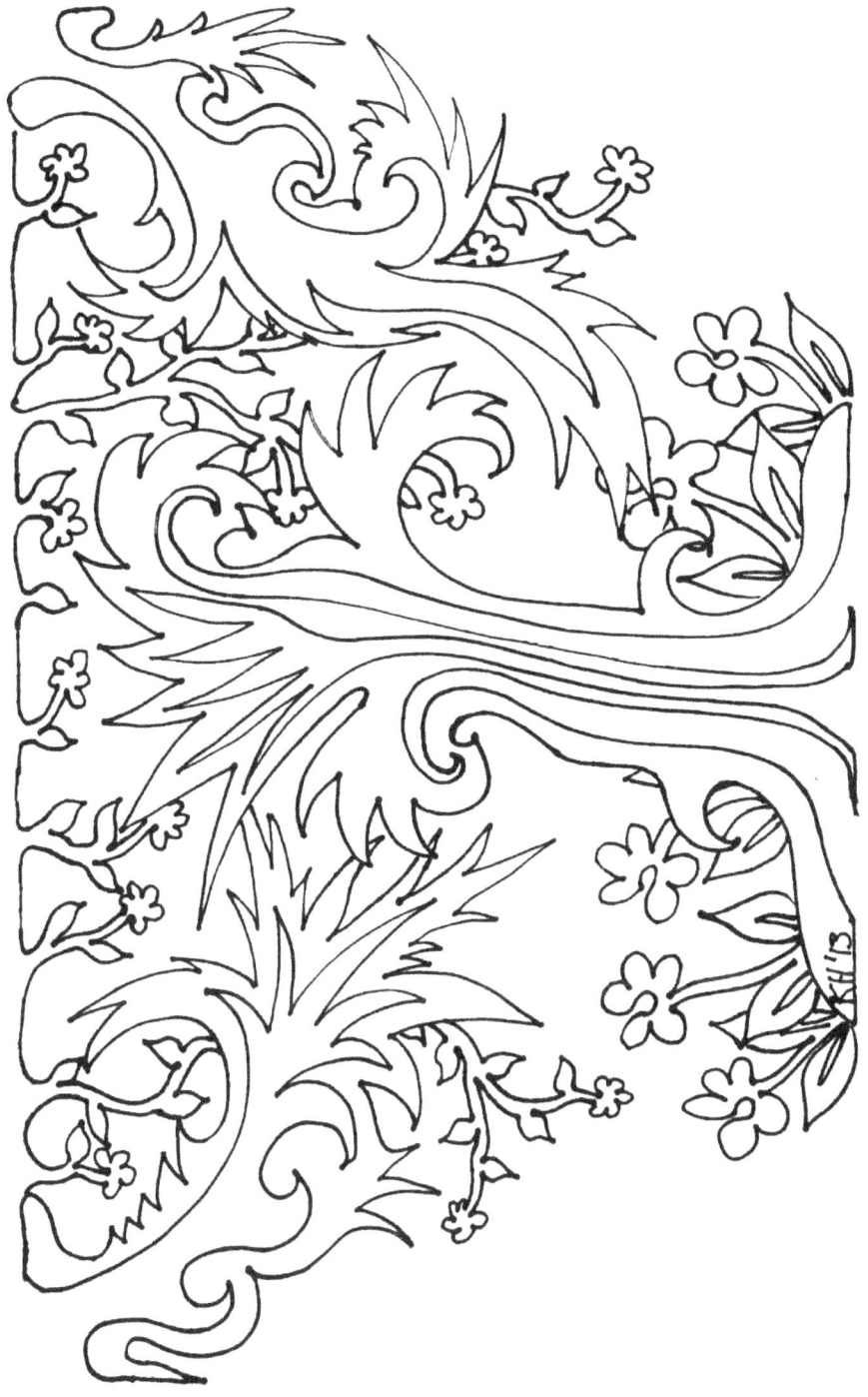

Kathy Carman Henderson

Flowers & Flair

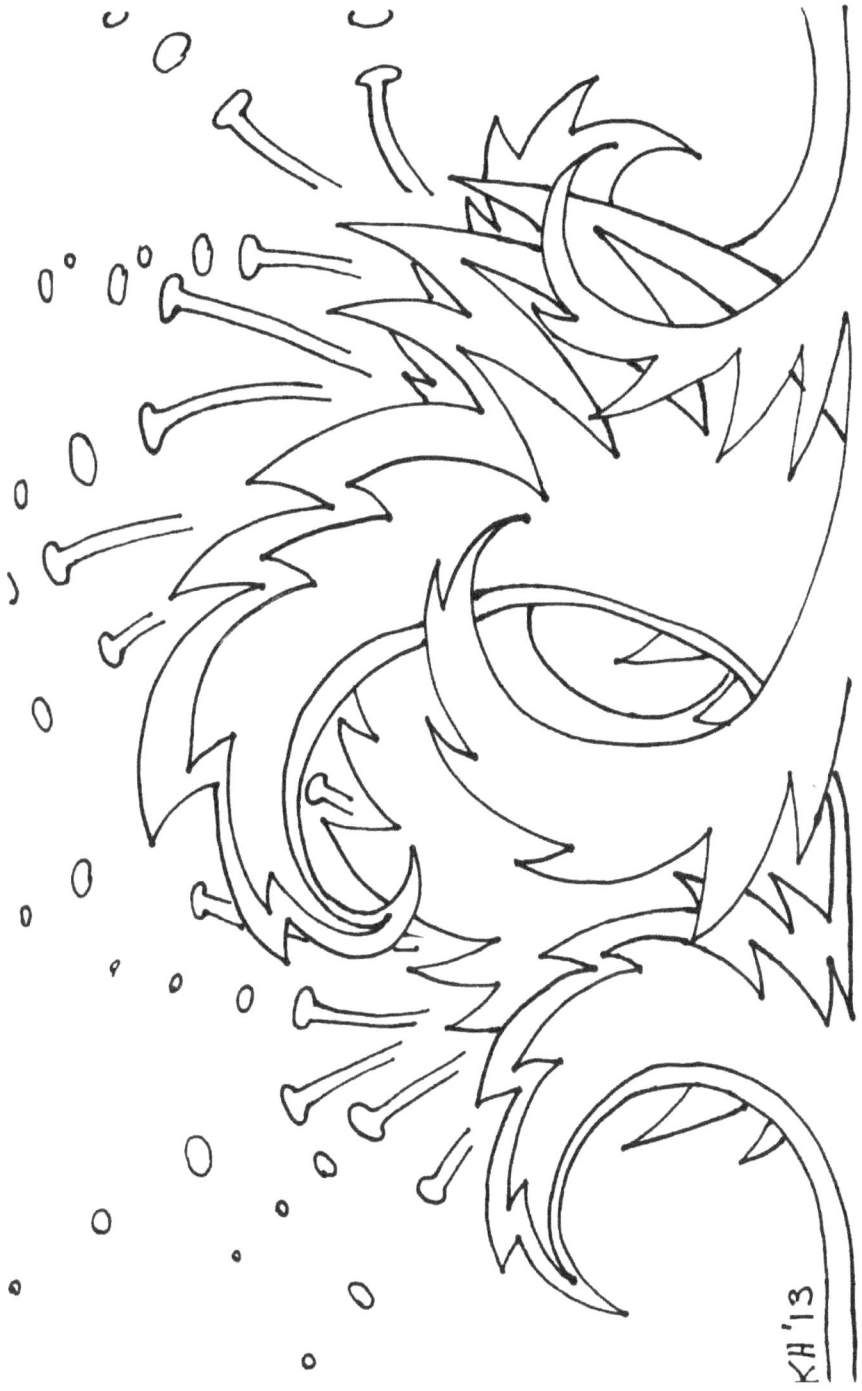

Kathy Carman Henderson

Flowers & Flair

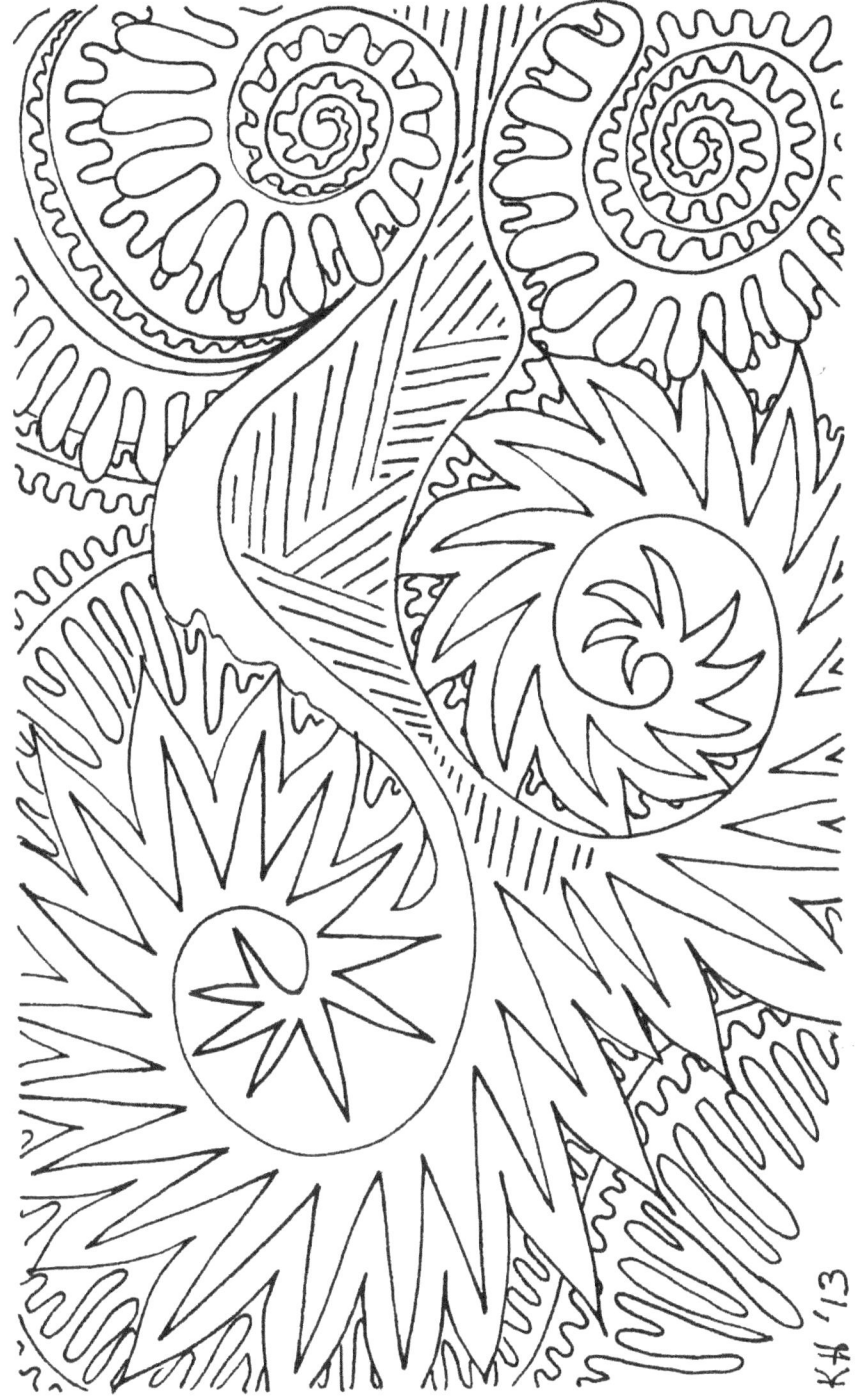

Kathy Carman Henderson

Flowers & Flair

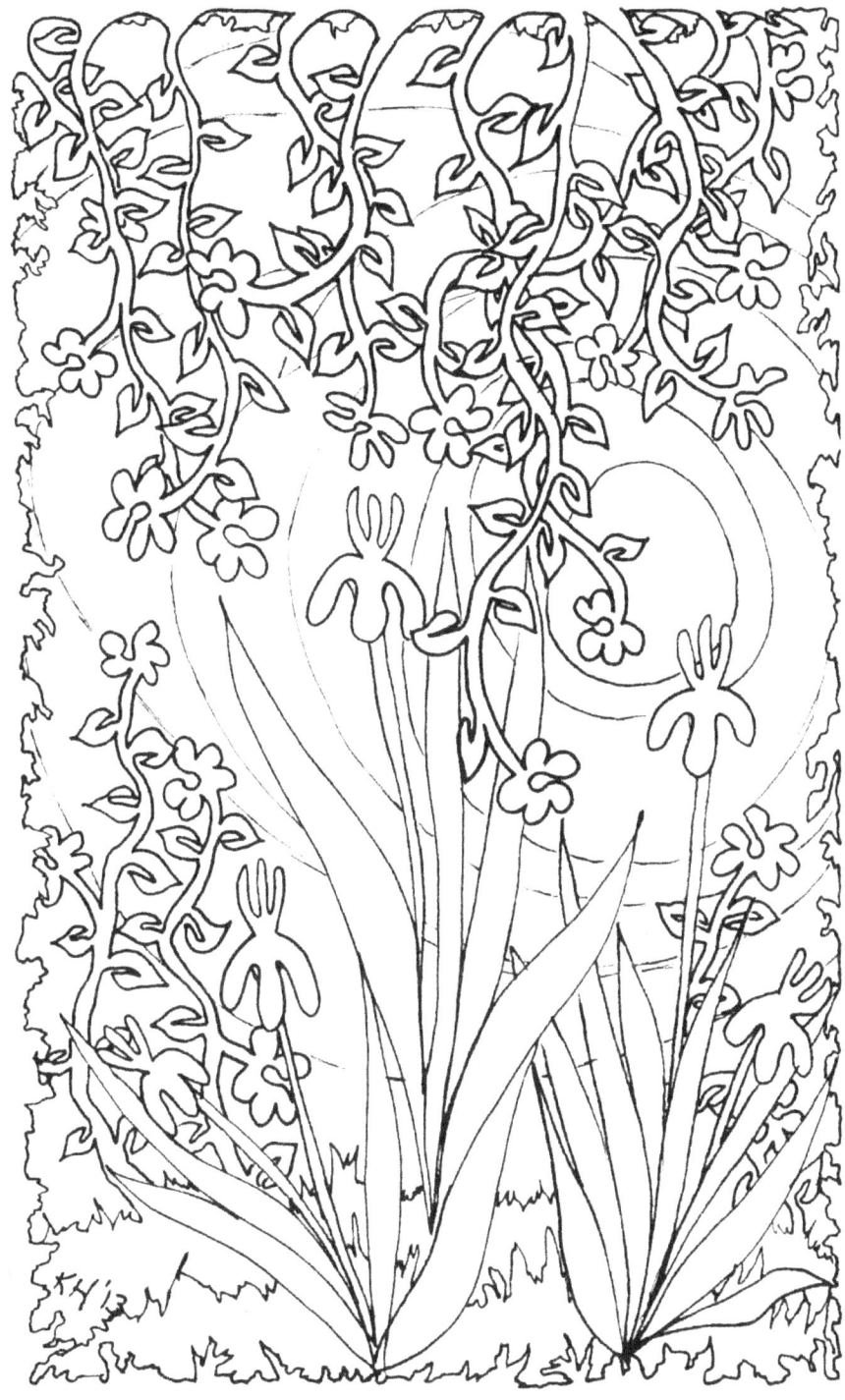

Kathy Carman Henderson

Flowers & Flair

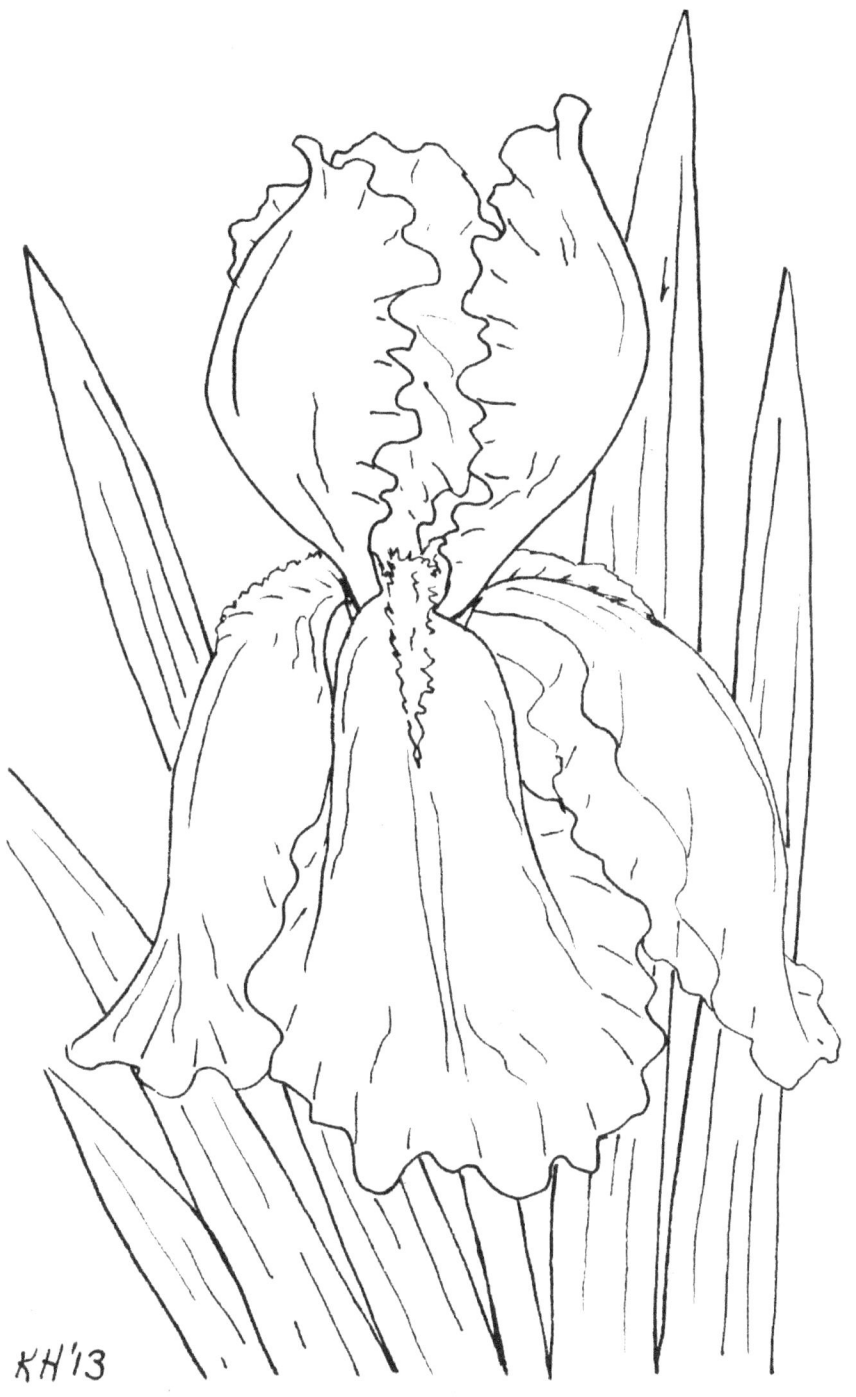

Kathy Carman Henderson

Flowers & Flair

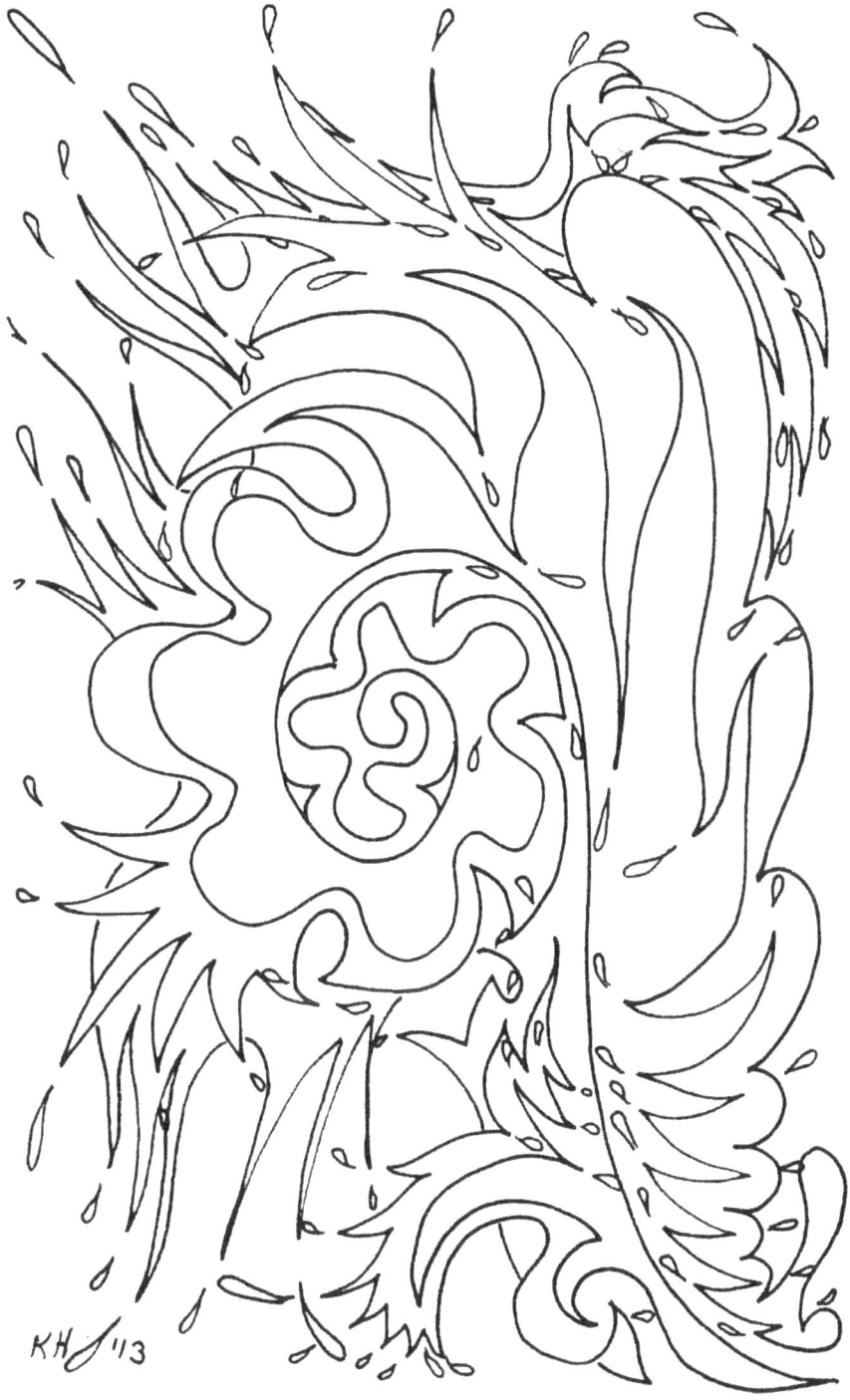

Kathy Carman Henderson

Flowers & Flair

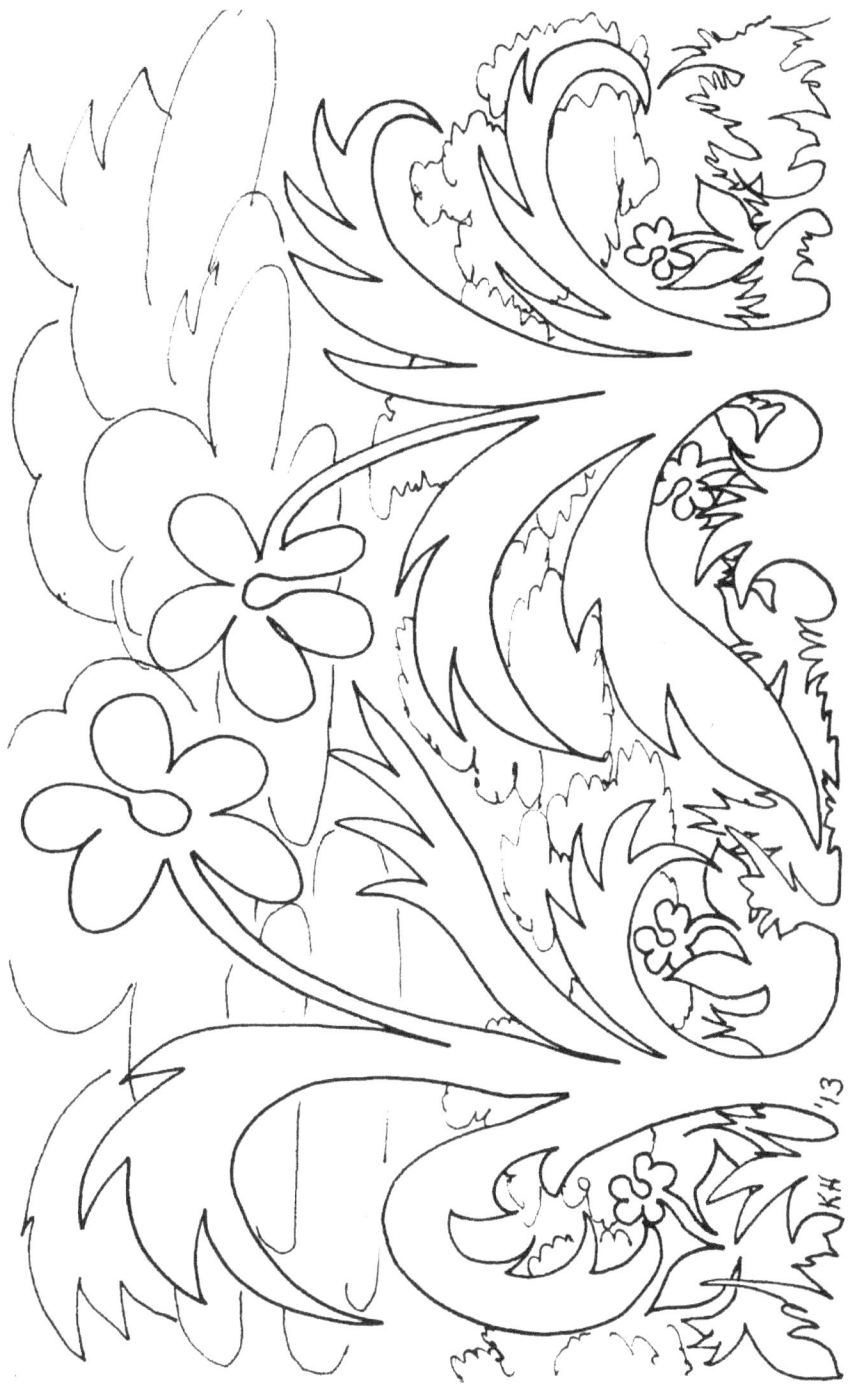

Kathy Carman Henderson

Flowers & Flair

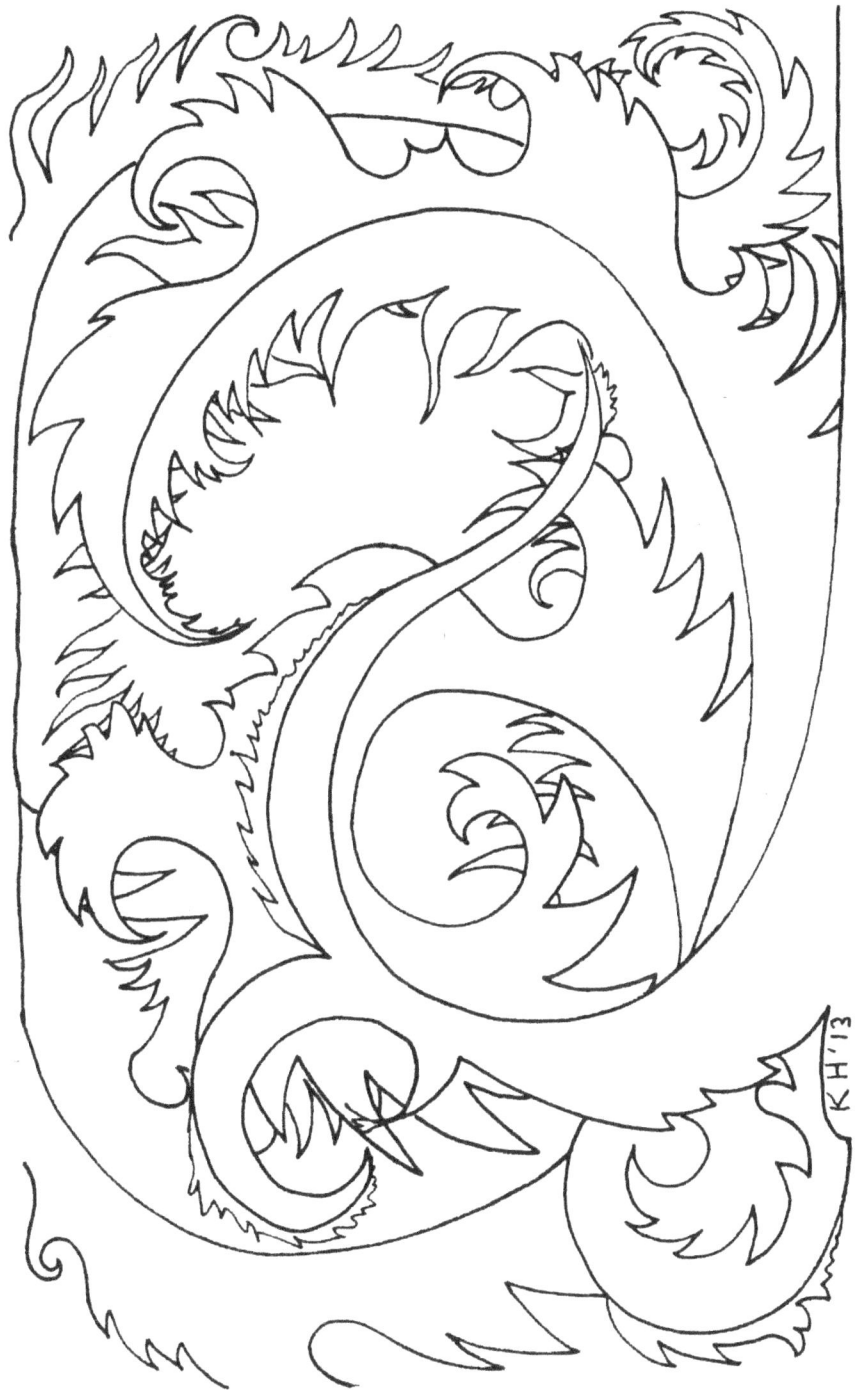

Kathy Carman Henderson

Flowers & Flair

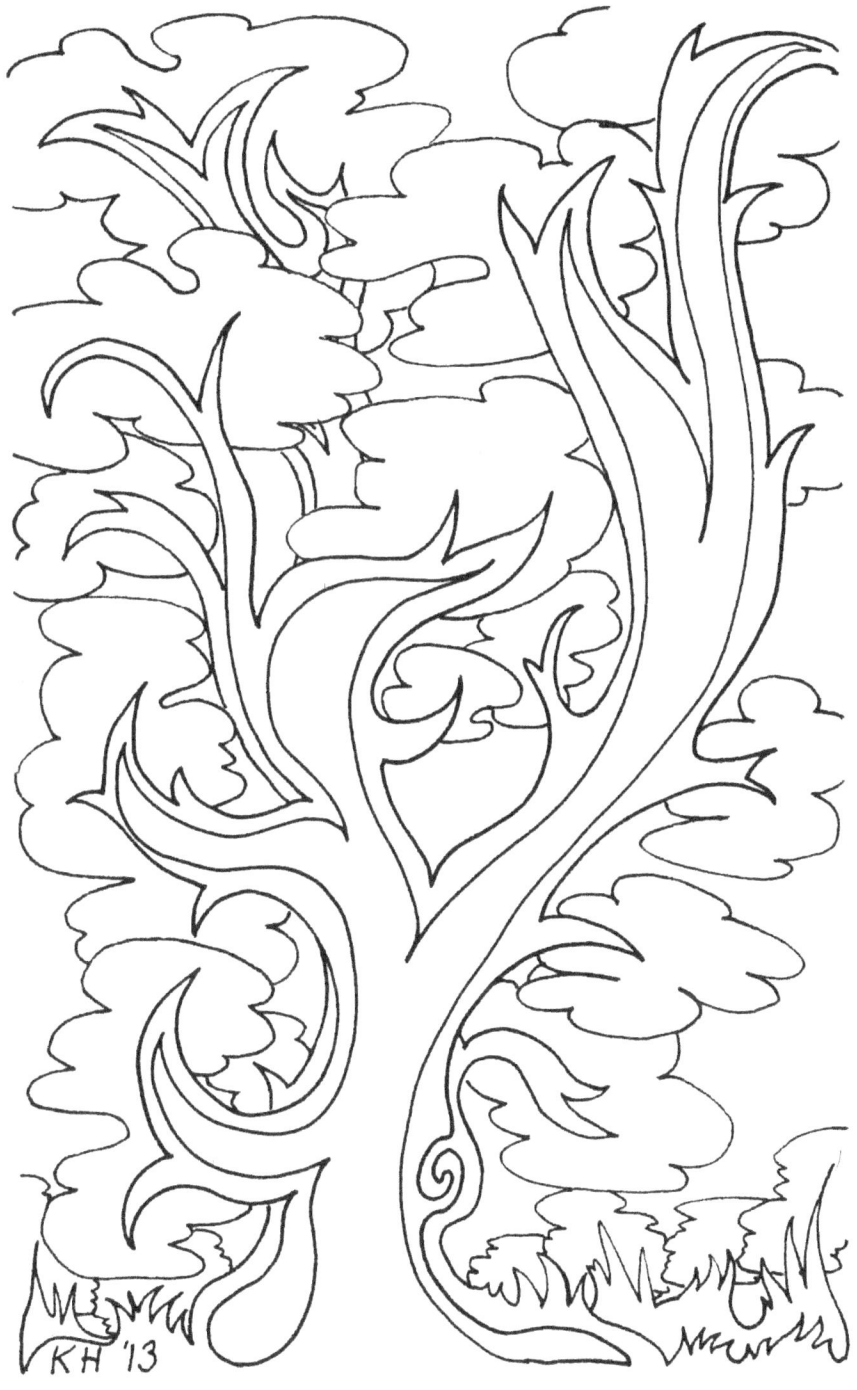

Kathy Carman Henderson

Flowers & Flair

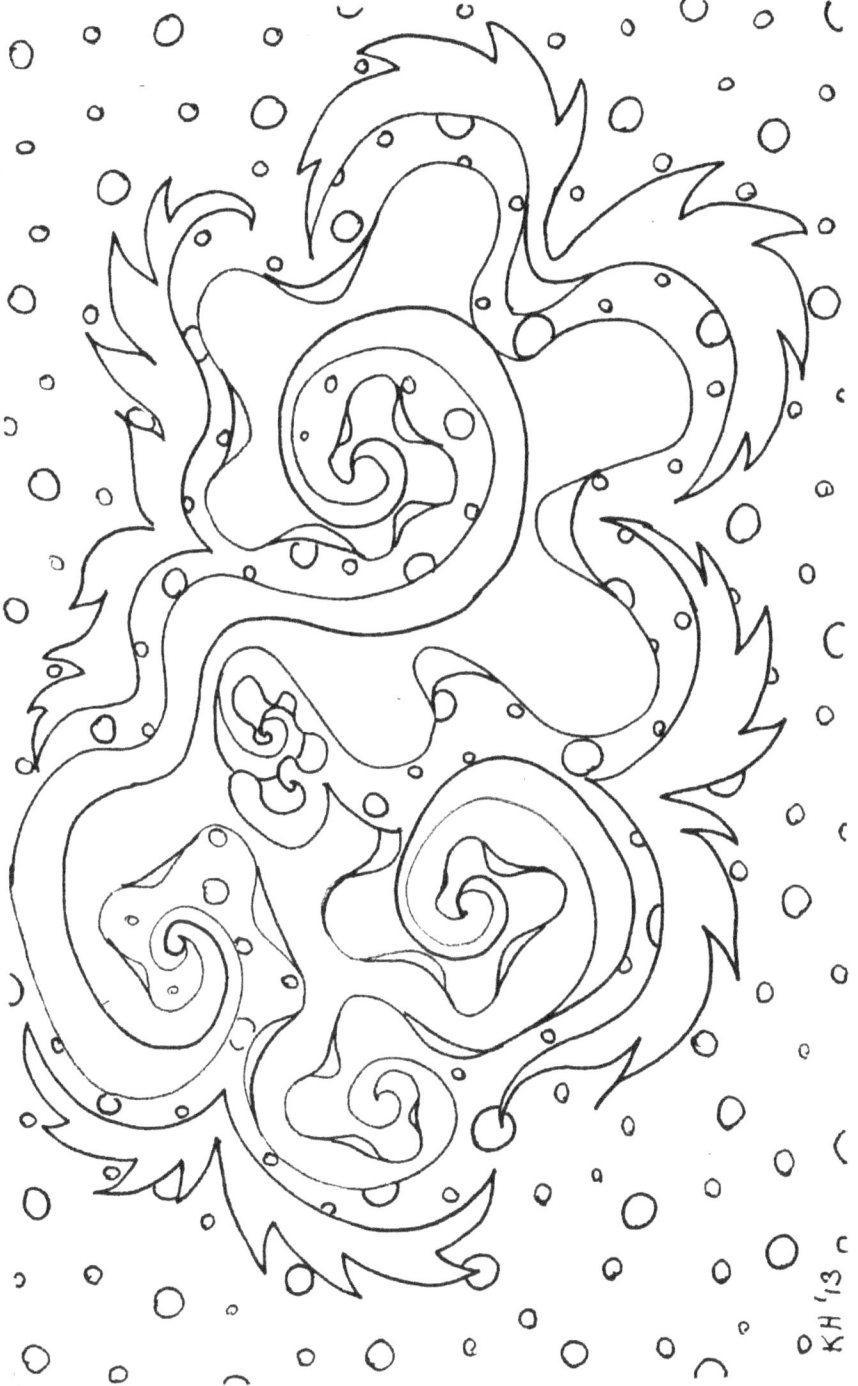

Kathy Carman Henderson

Flowers & Flair

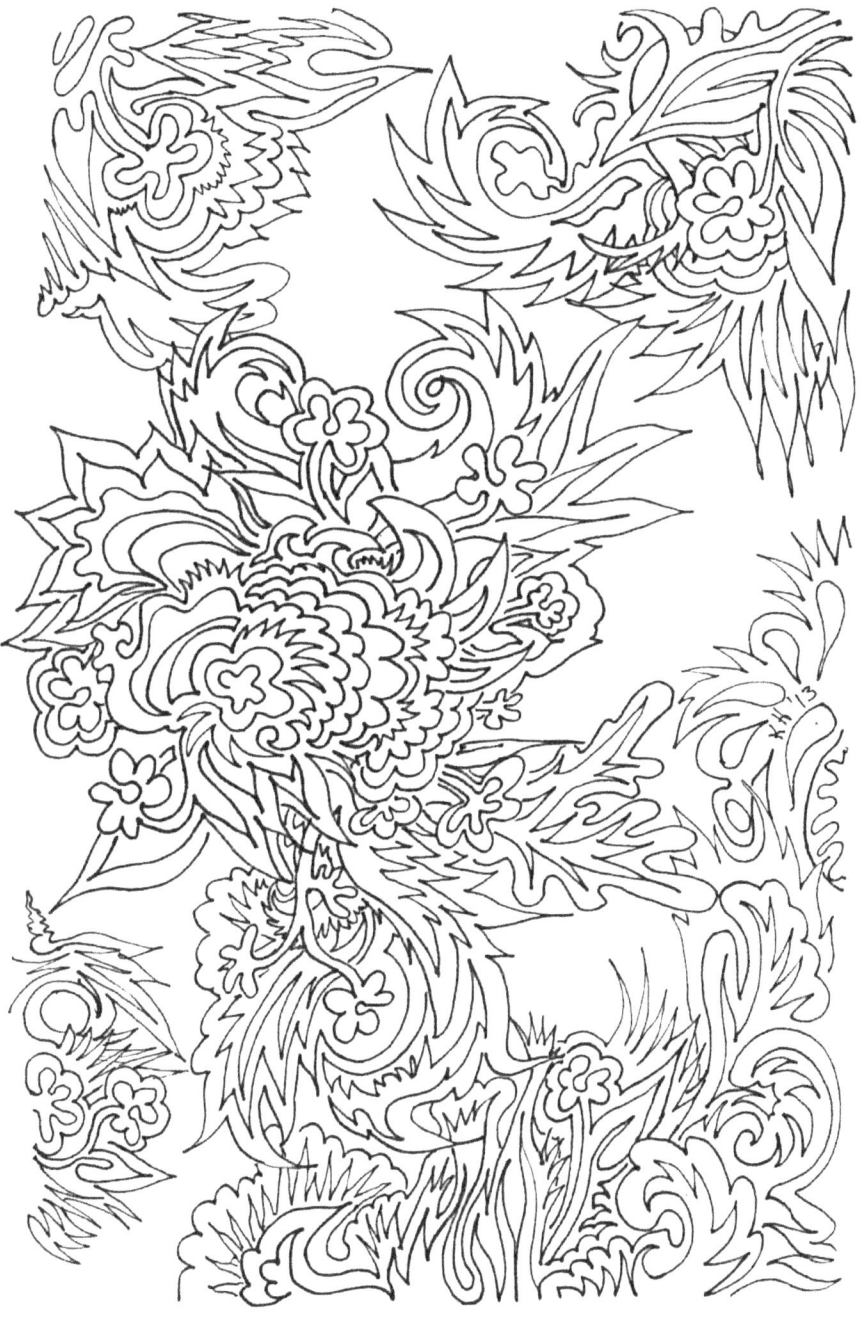

Kathy Carman Henderson

Flowers & Flair

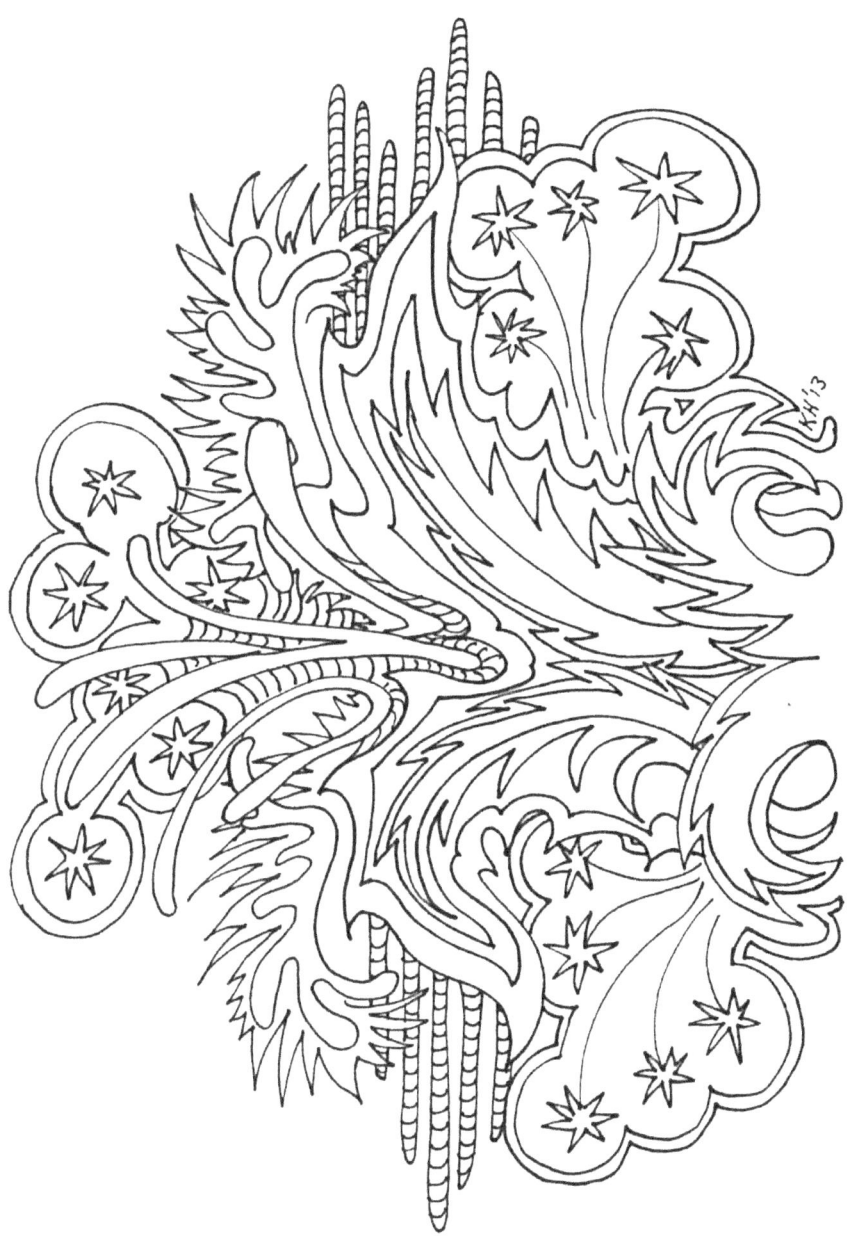

Kathy Carman Henderson

Flowers & Flair

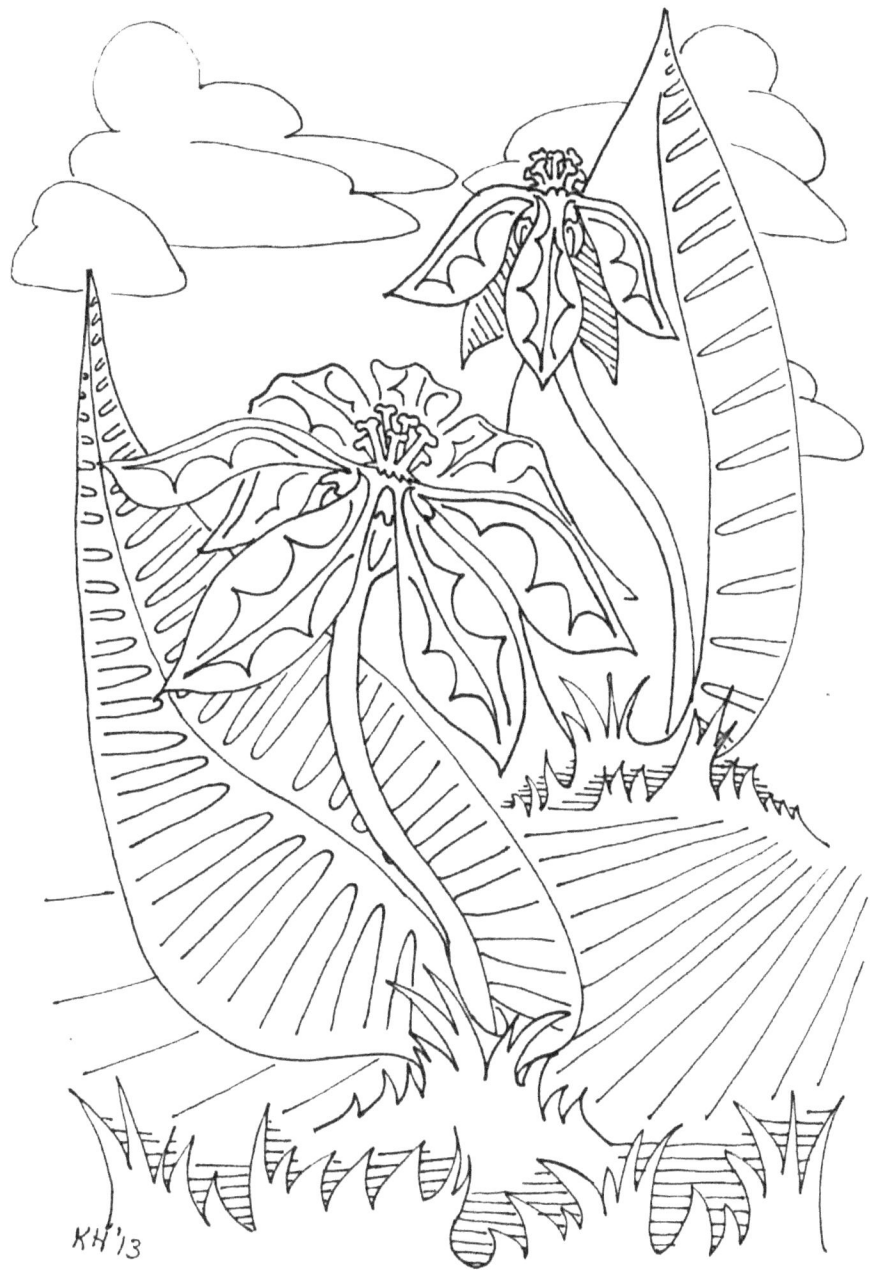

Kathy Carman Henderson

Flowers & Flair

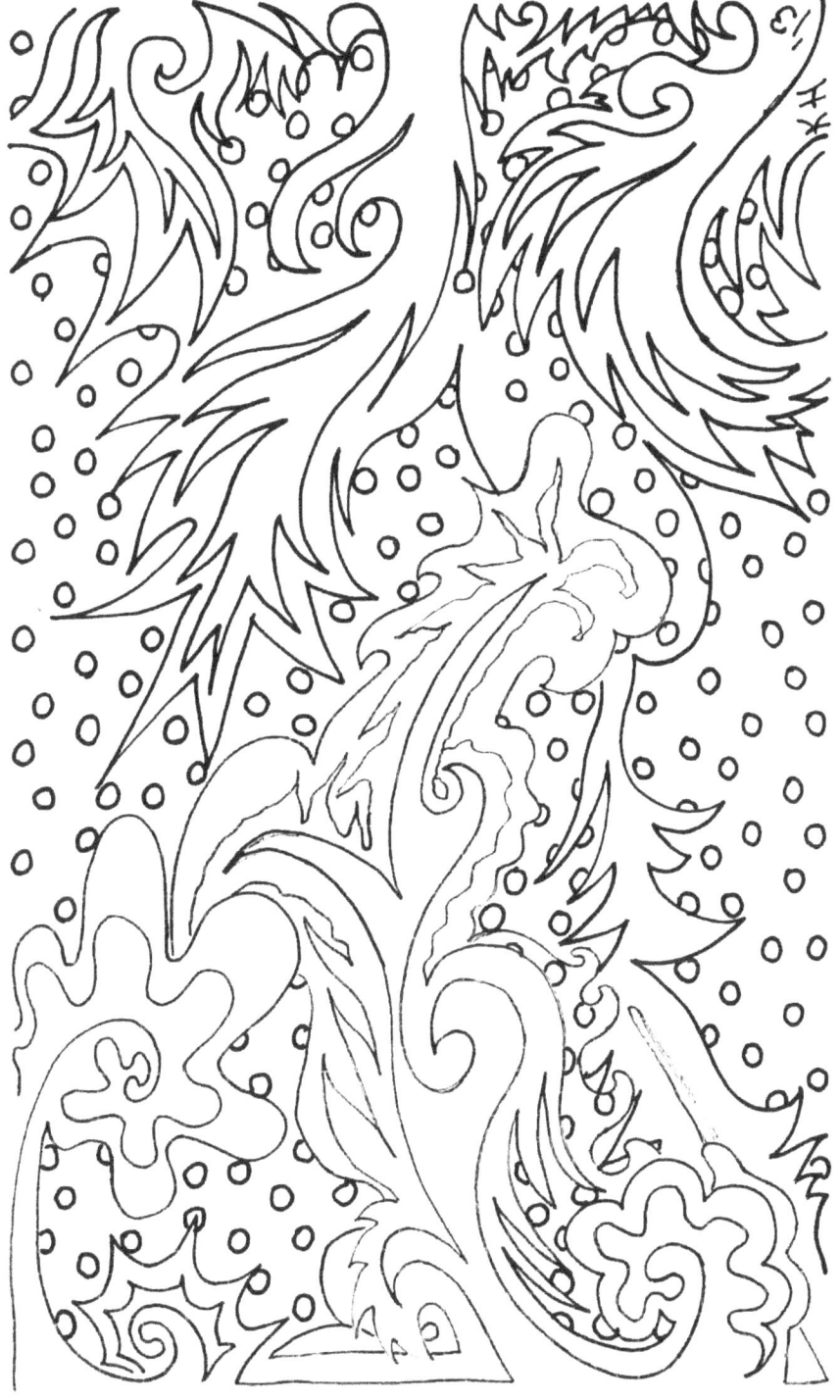

Kathy Carman Henderson

Flowers & Flair

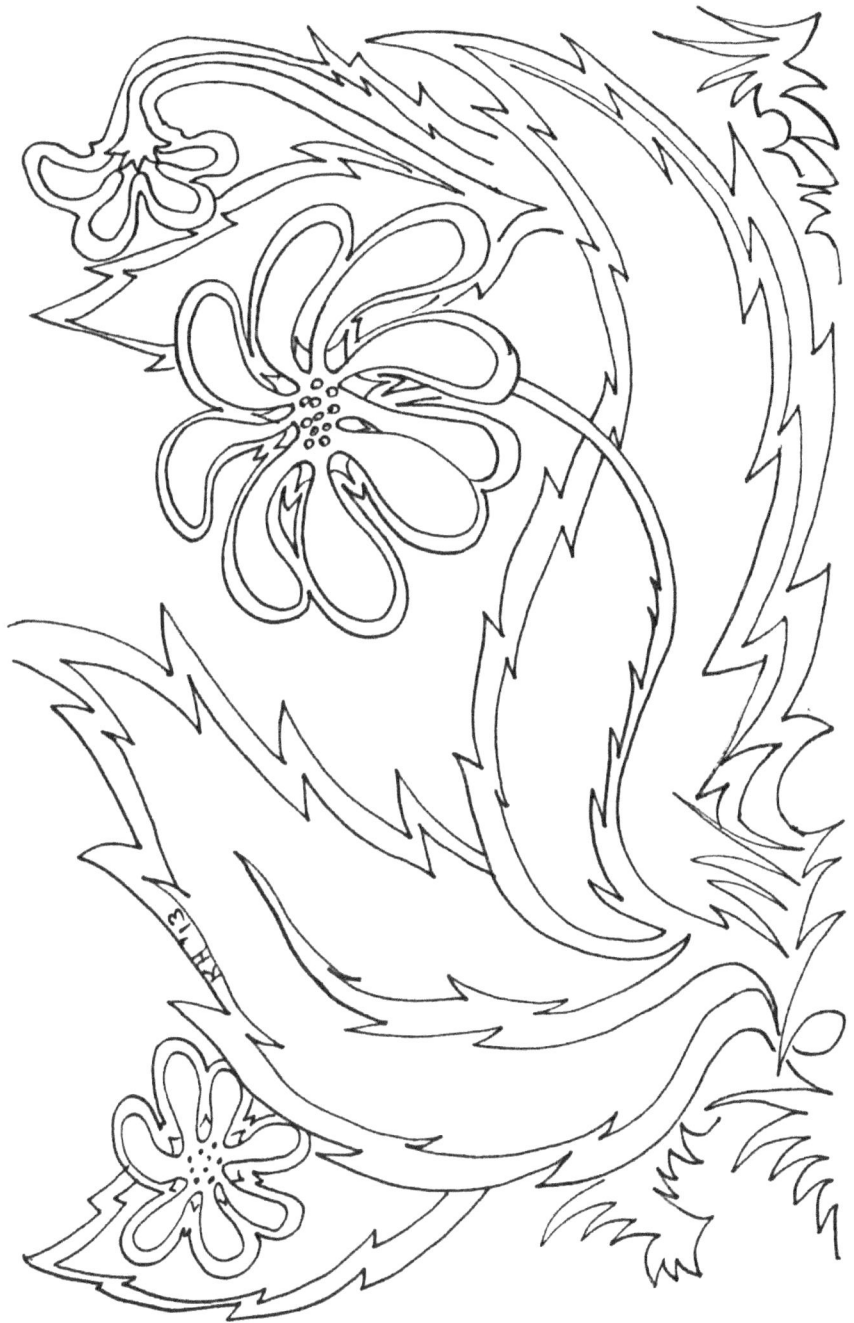

Kathy Carman Henderson

Flowers & Flair

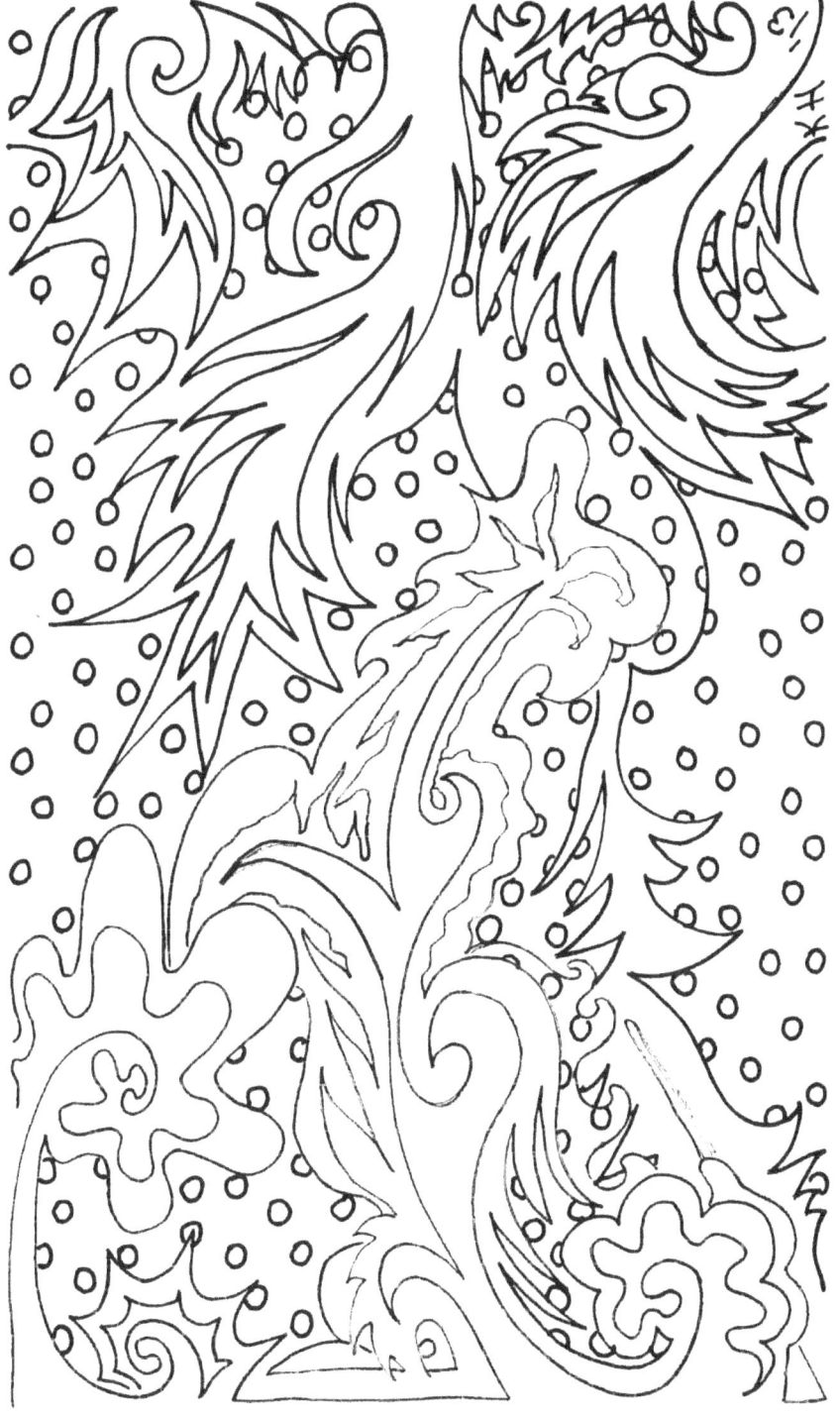

Kathy Carman Henderson

Flowers & Flair

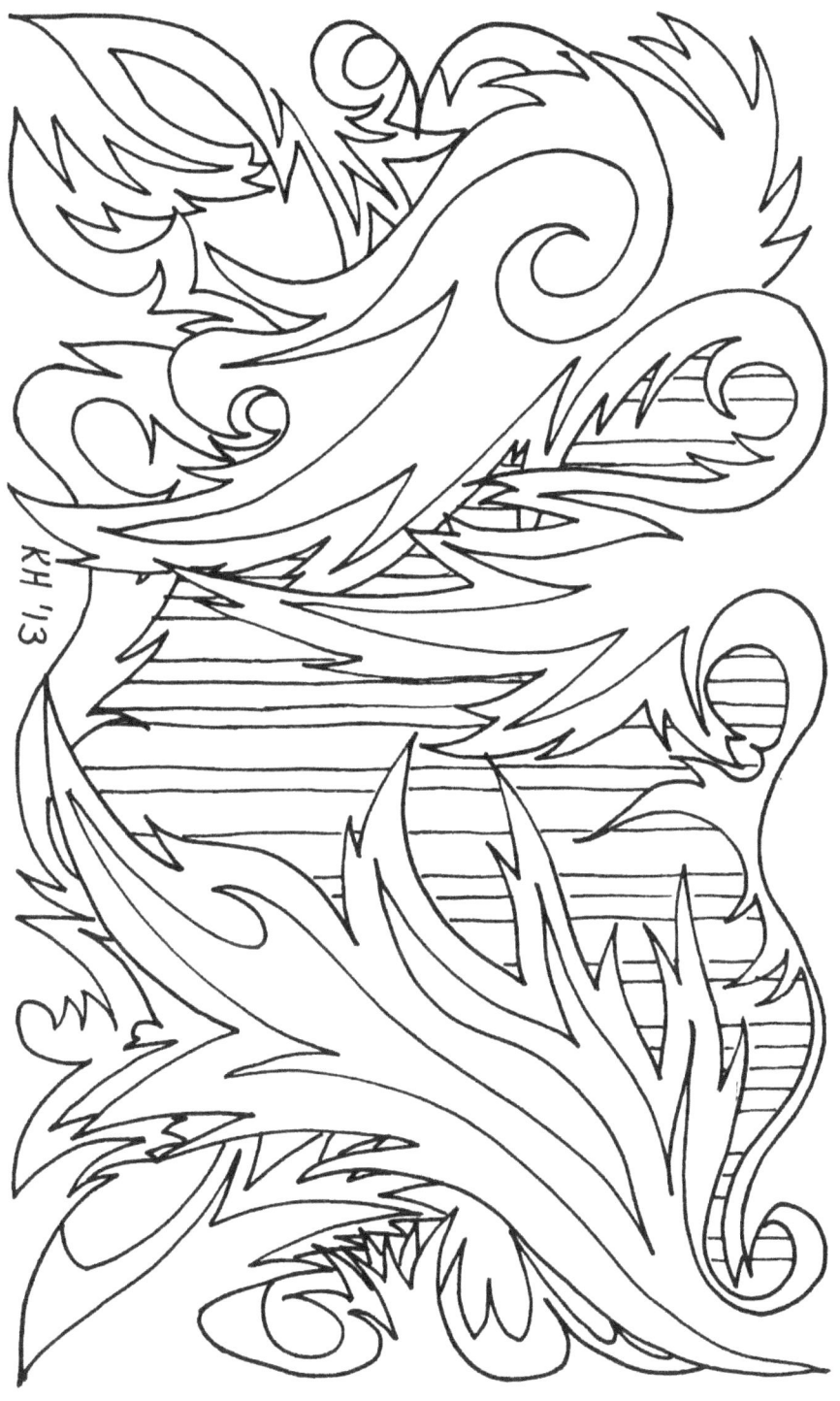

Kathy Carman Henderson

Flowers & Flair

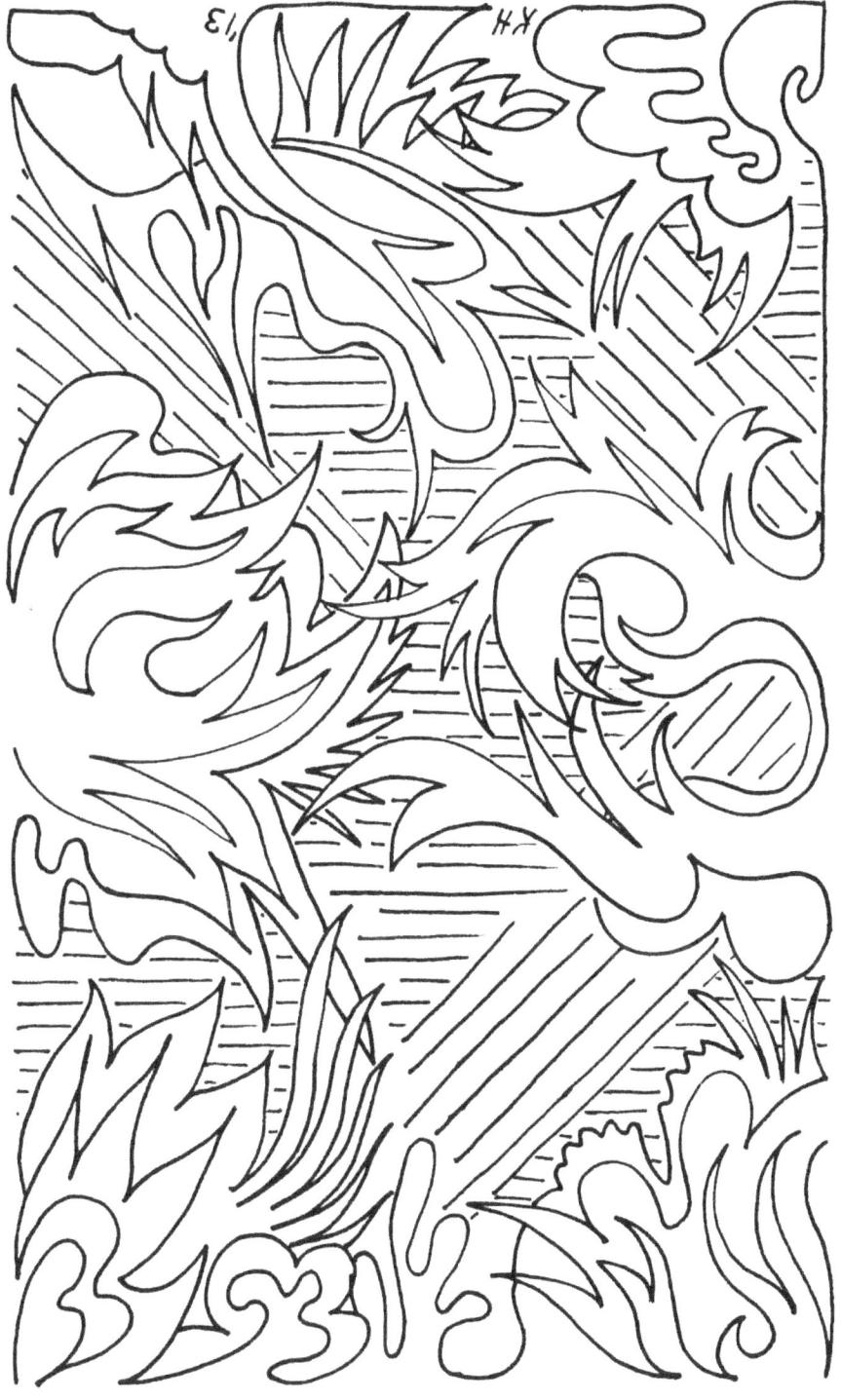

Kathy Carman Henderson

Flowers & Flair

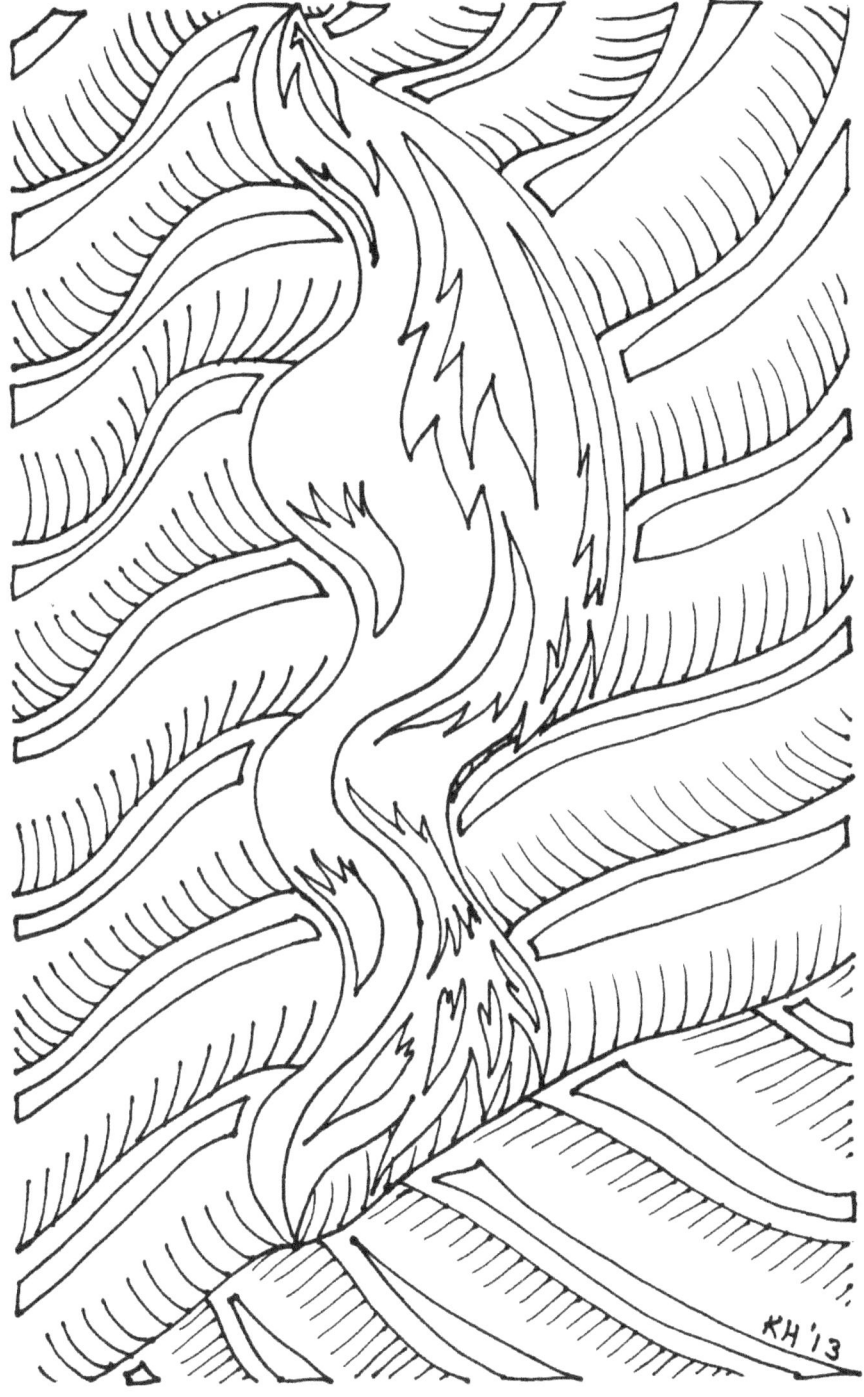

Kathy Carman Henderson

Flowers & Flair

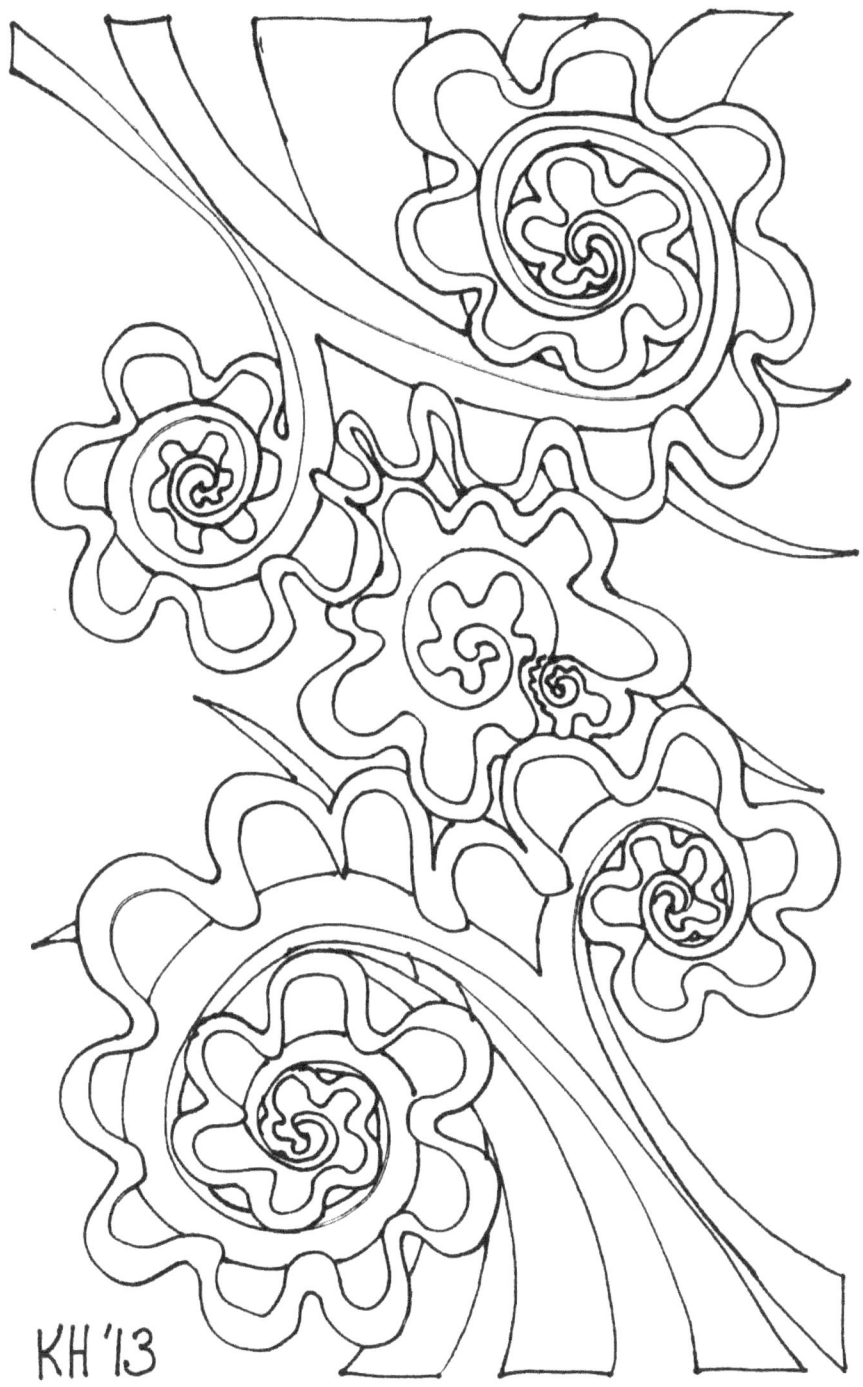

Kathy Carman Henderson

Flowers & Flair

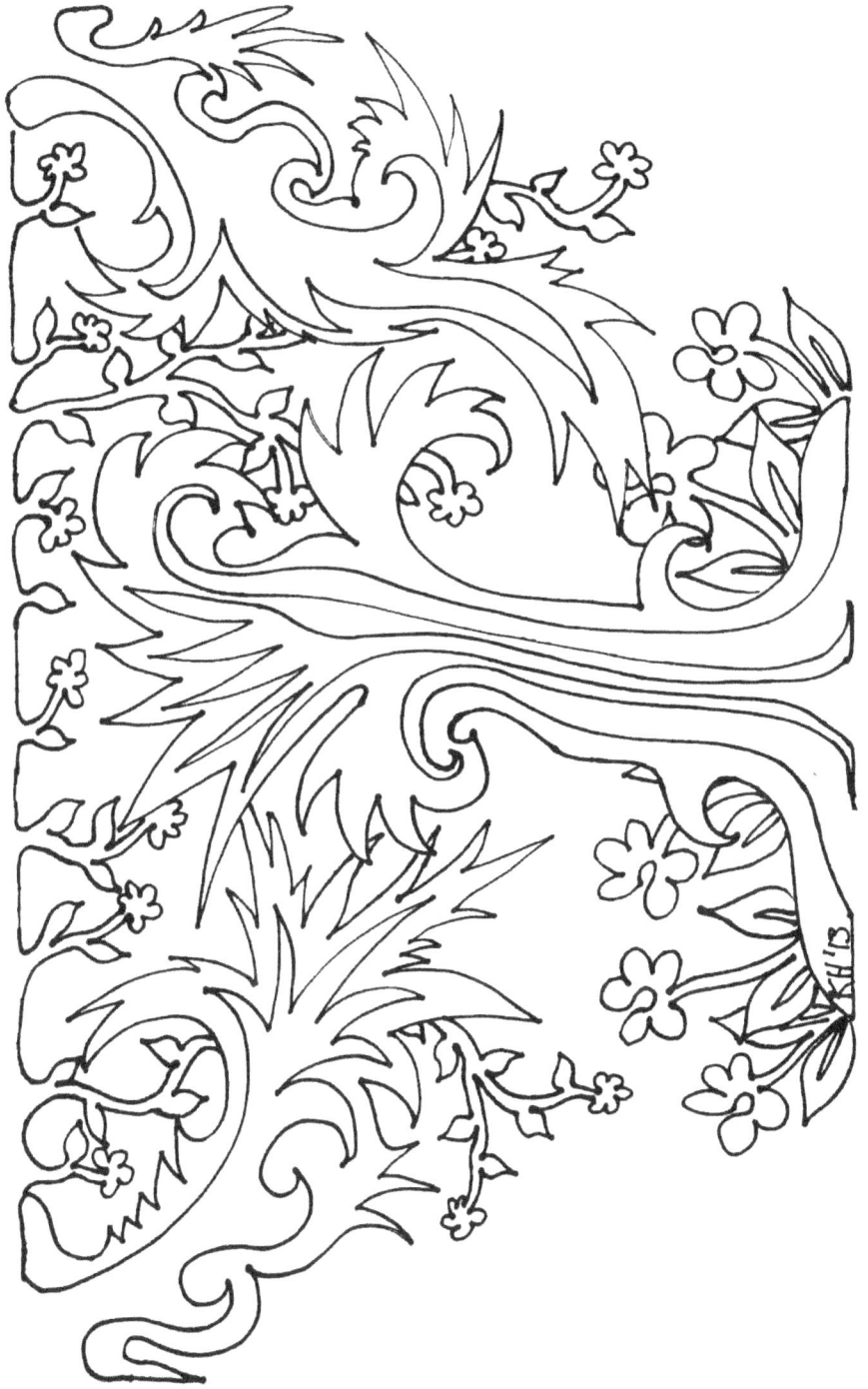

Kathy Carman Henderson

Flowers & Flair

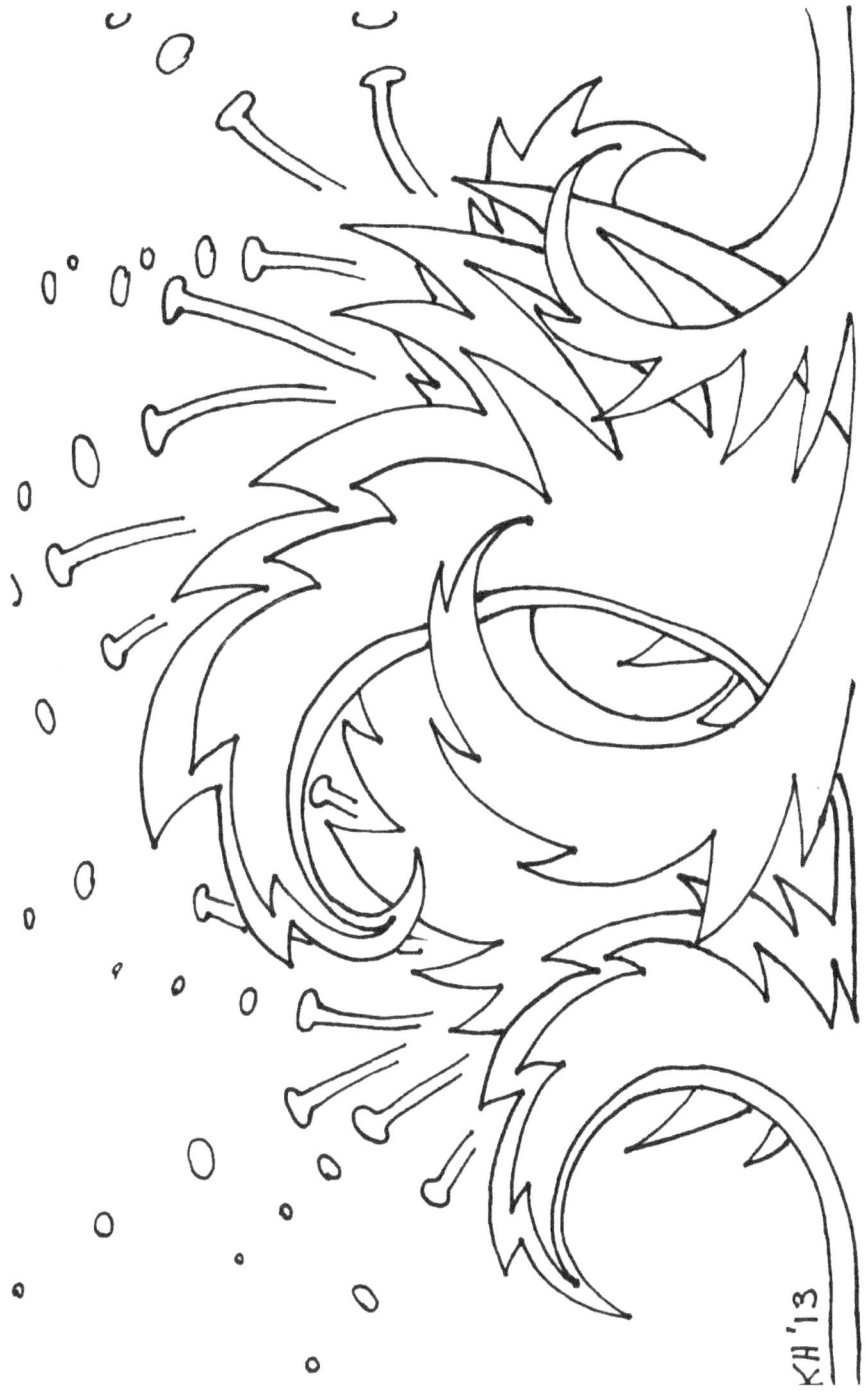

Kathy Carman Henderson

Flowers & Flair

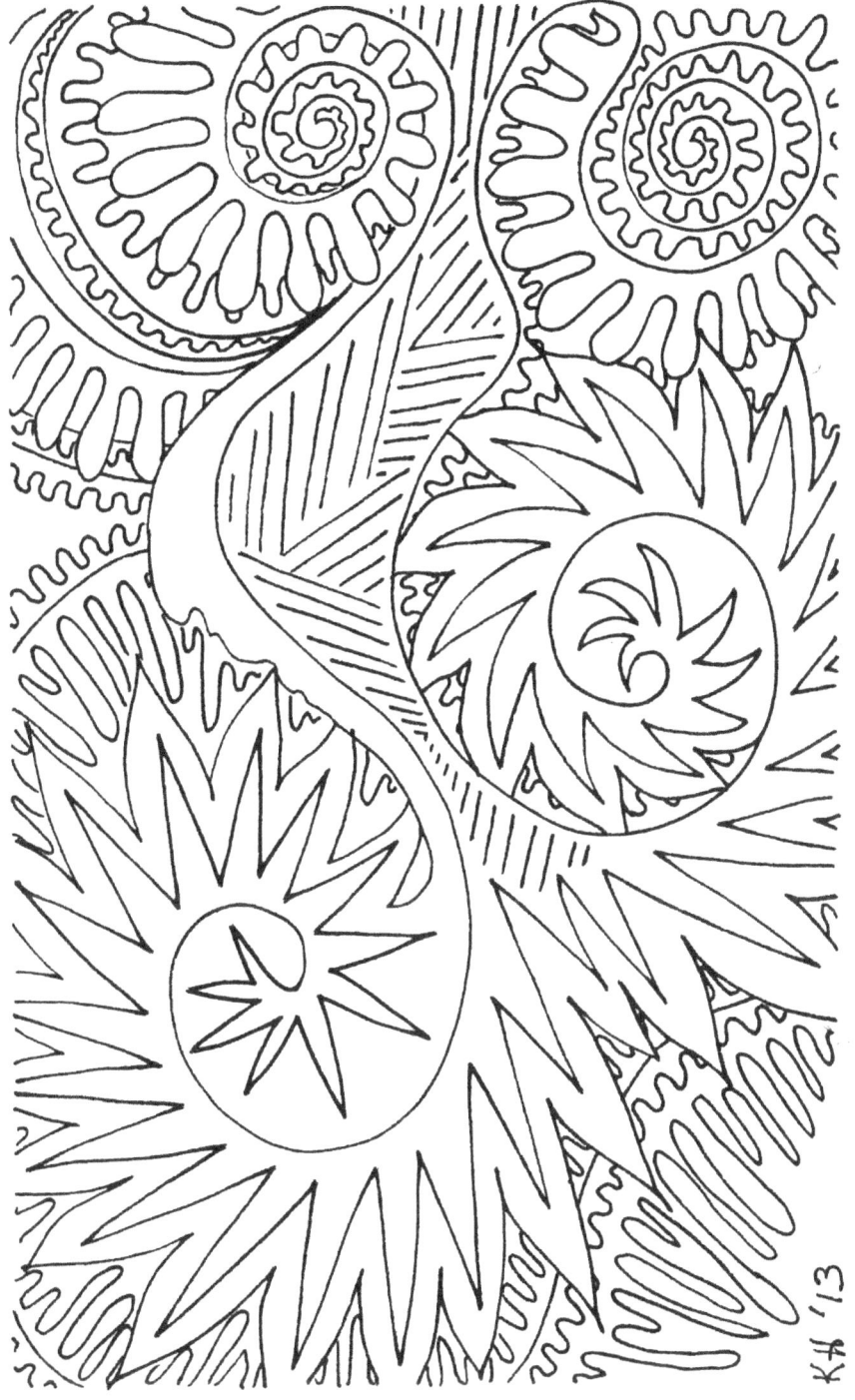

Kathy Carman Henderson

Flowers & Flair

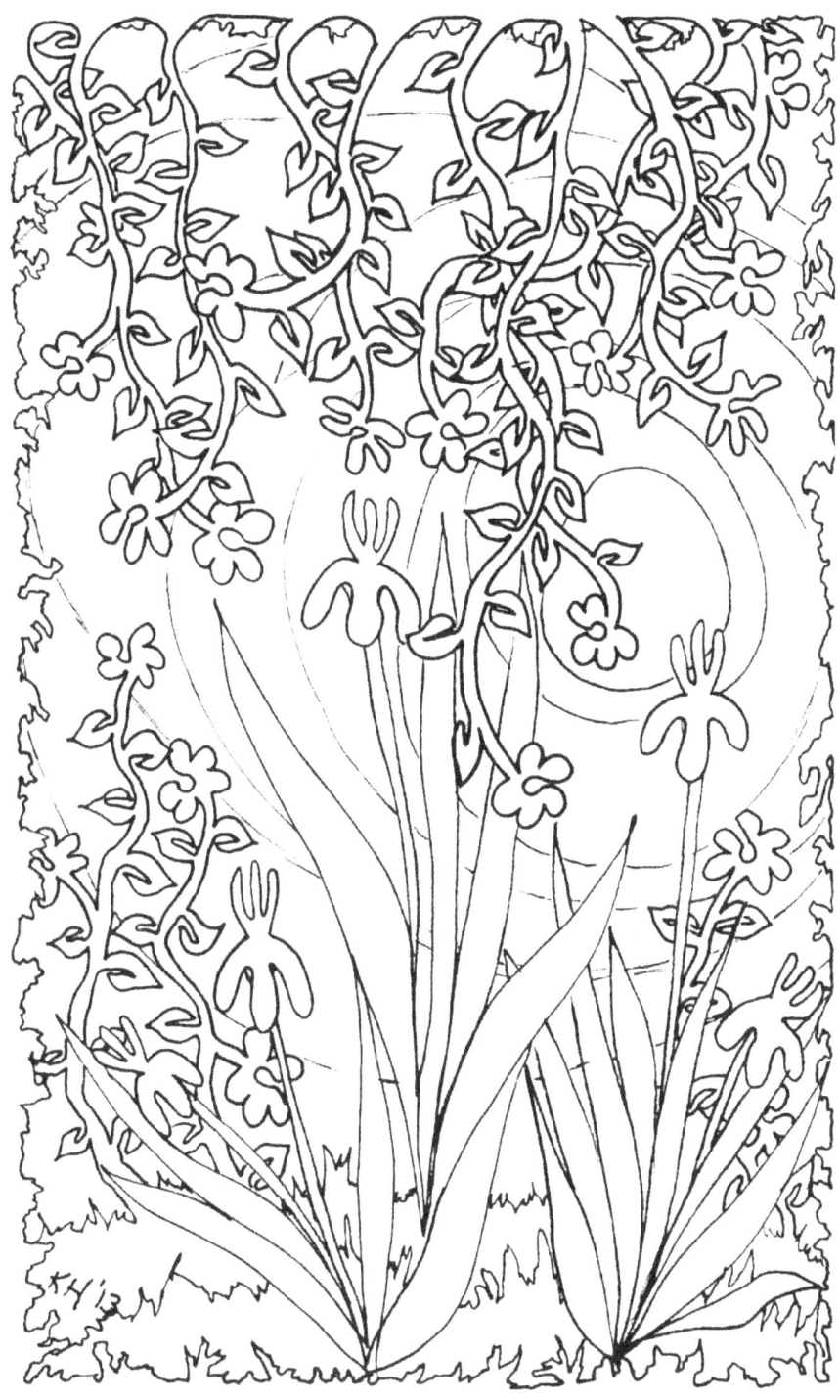

Kathy Carman Henderson

Flowers & Flair

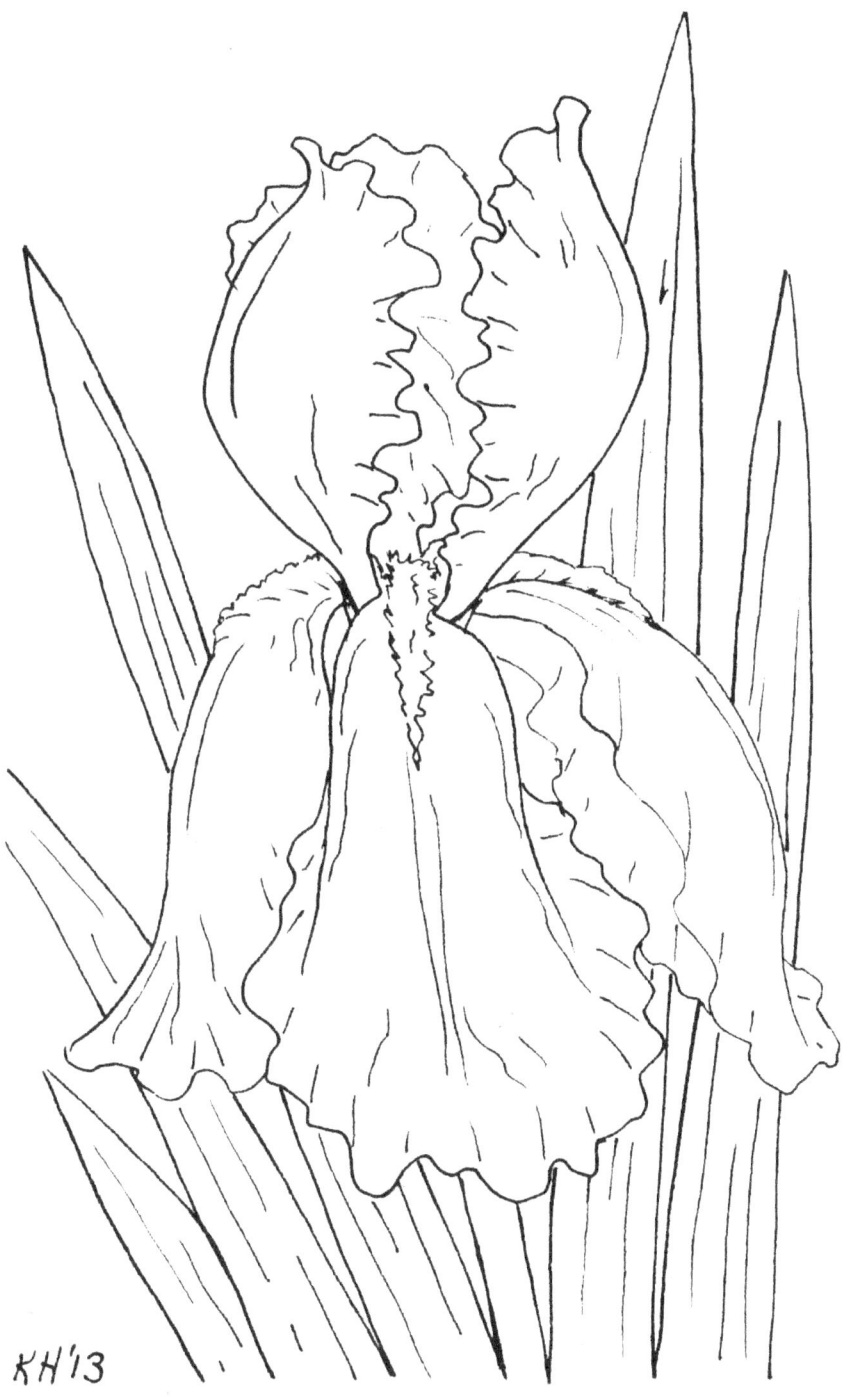

Kathy Carman Henderson

Flowers & Flair

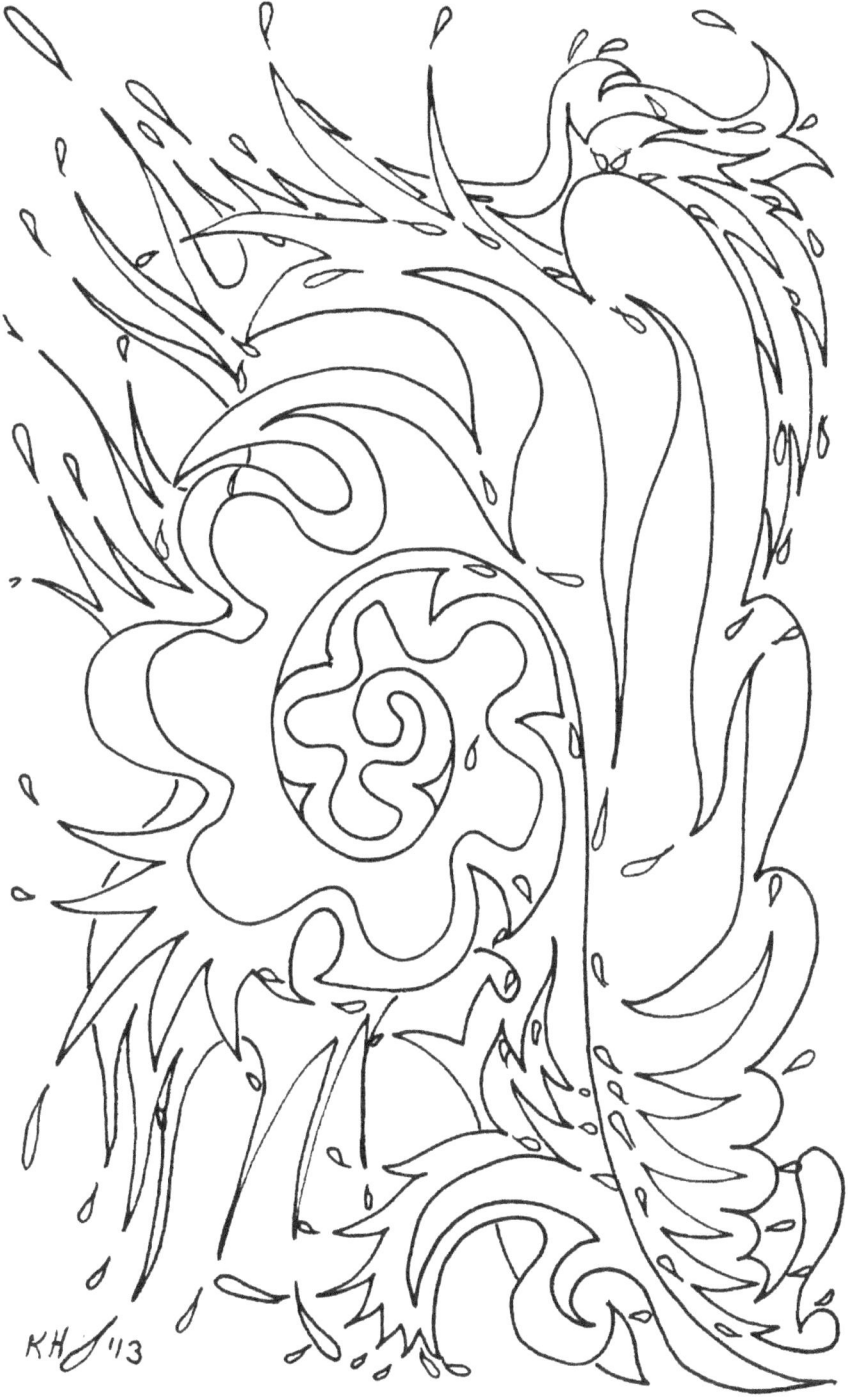

Kathy Carman Henderson

Flowers & Flair

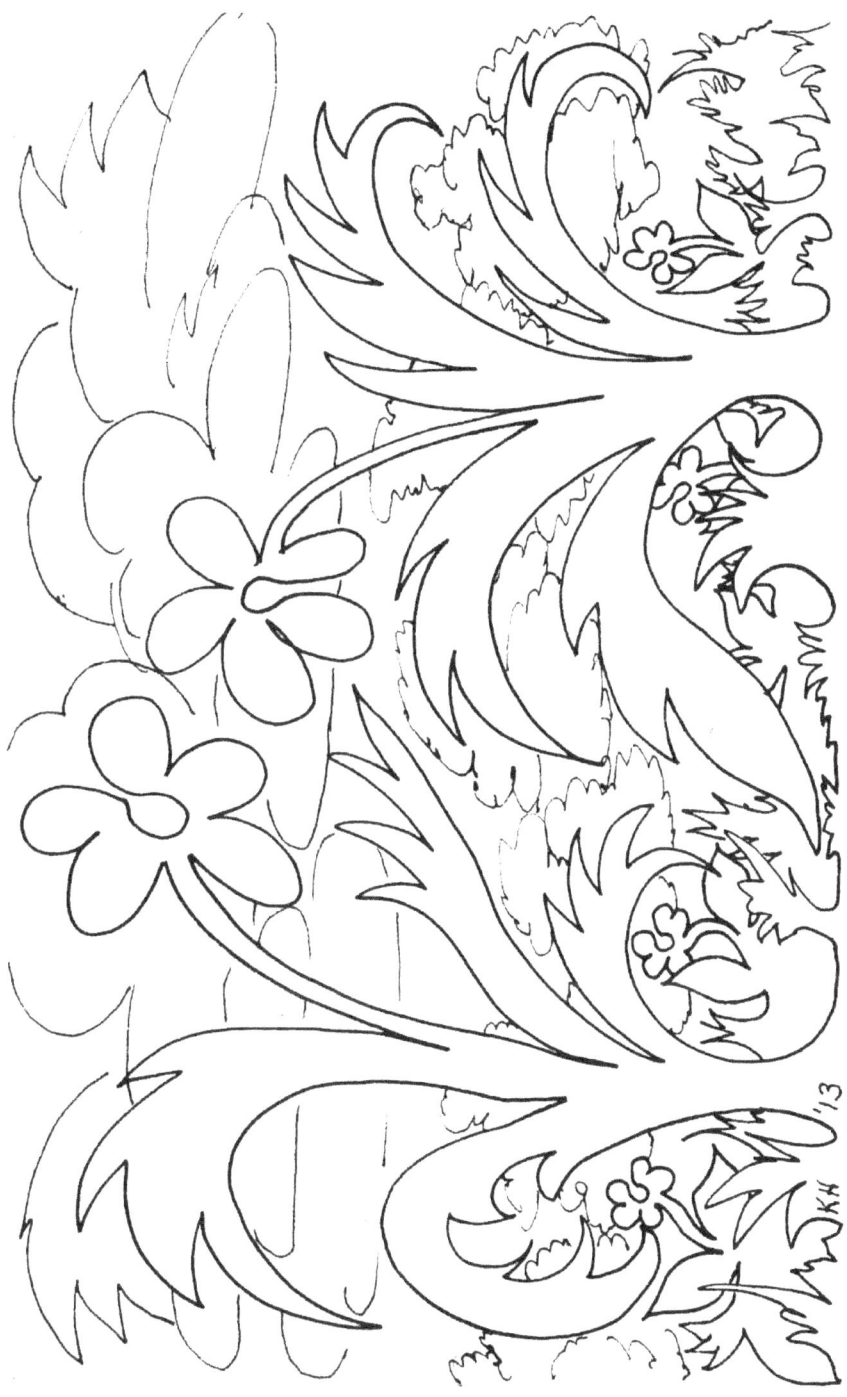

Kathy Carman Henderson

Flowers & Flair

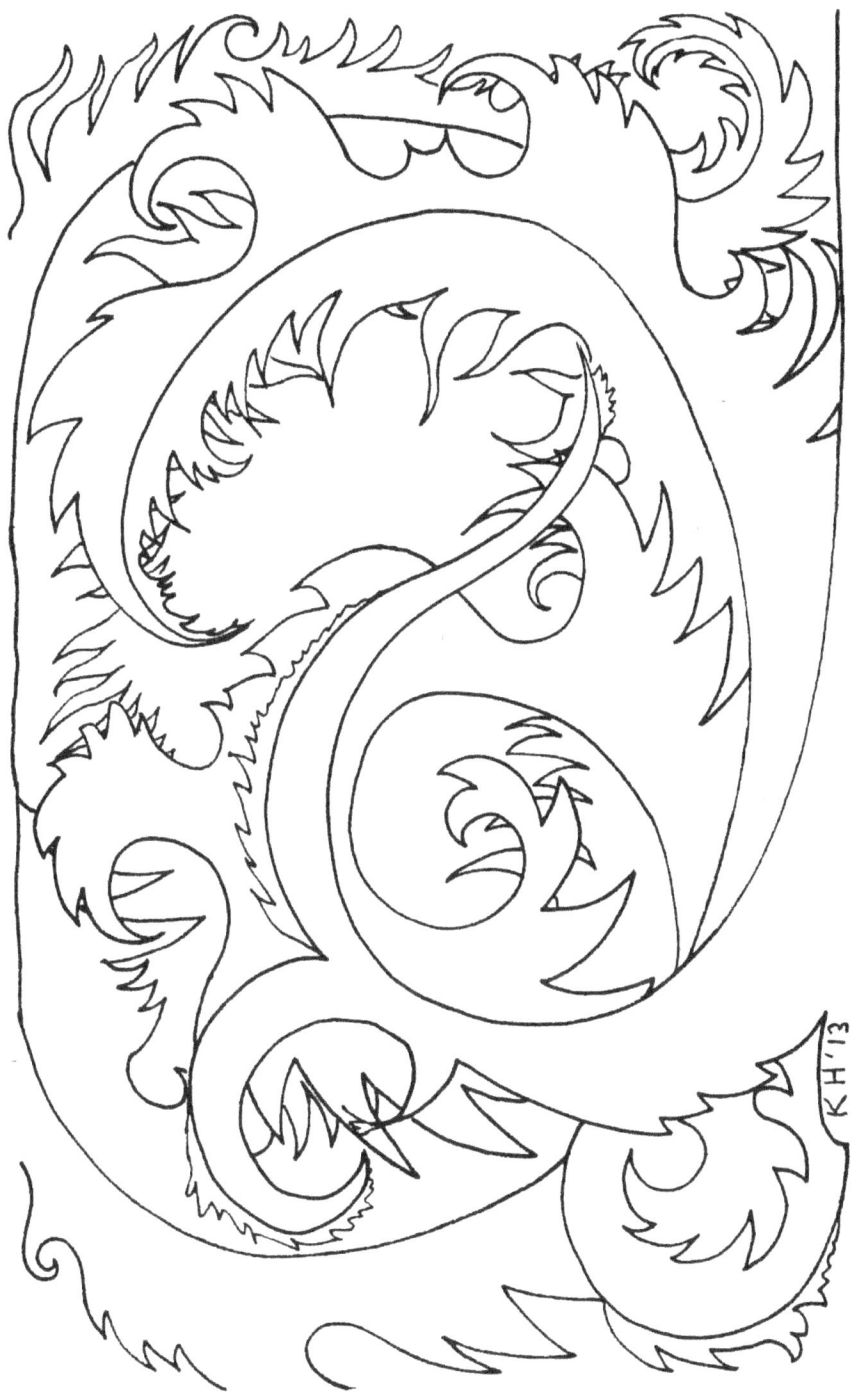

Kathy Carman Henderson

Flowers & Flair

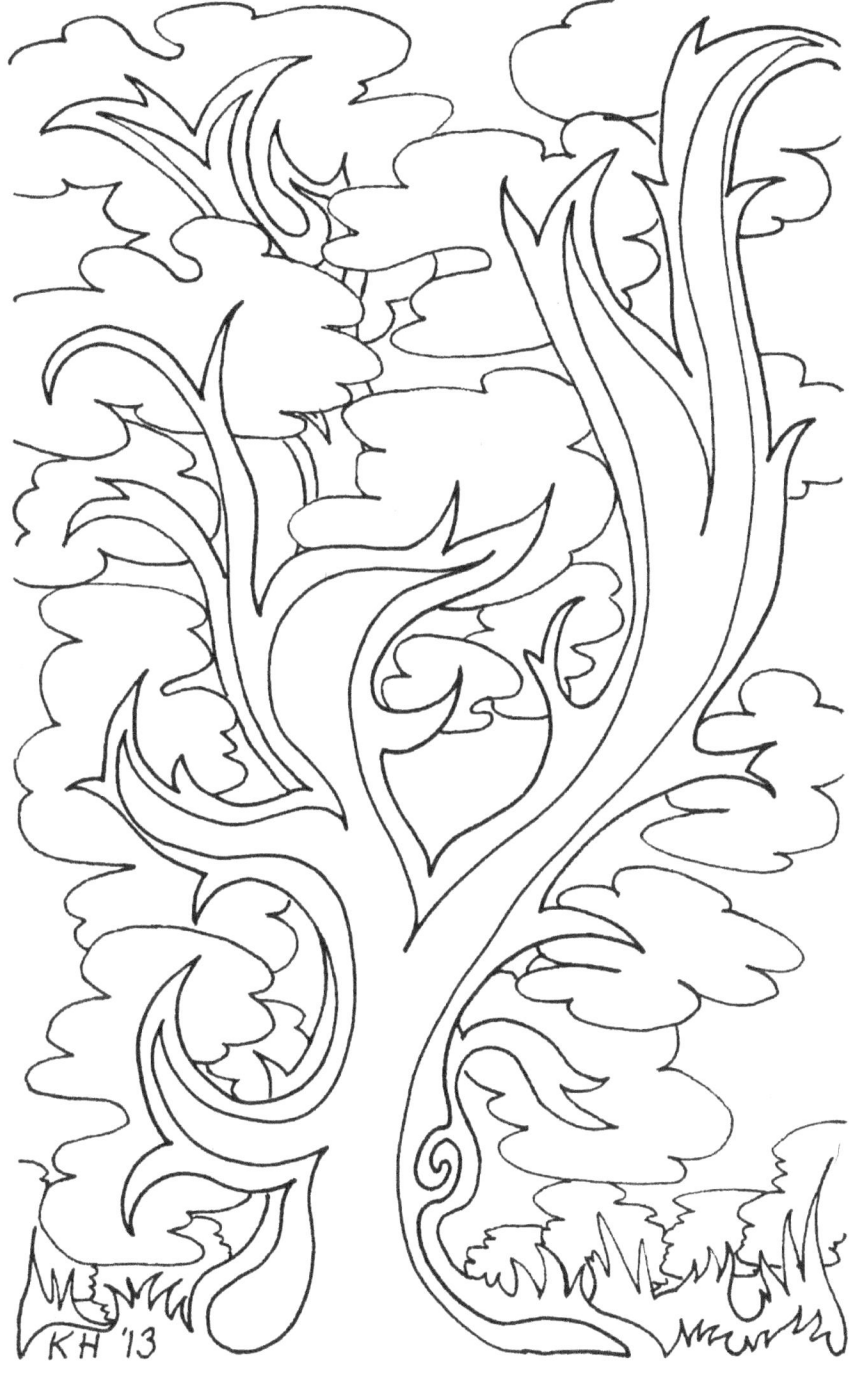

Kathy Carman Henderson

Flowers & Flair

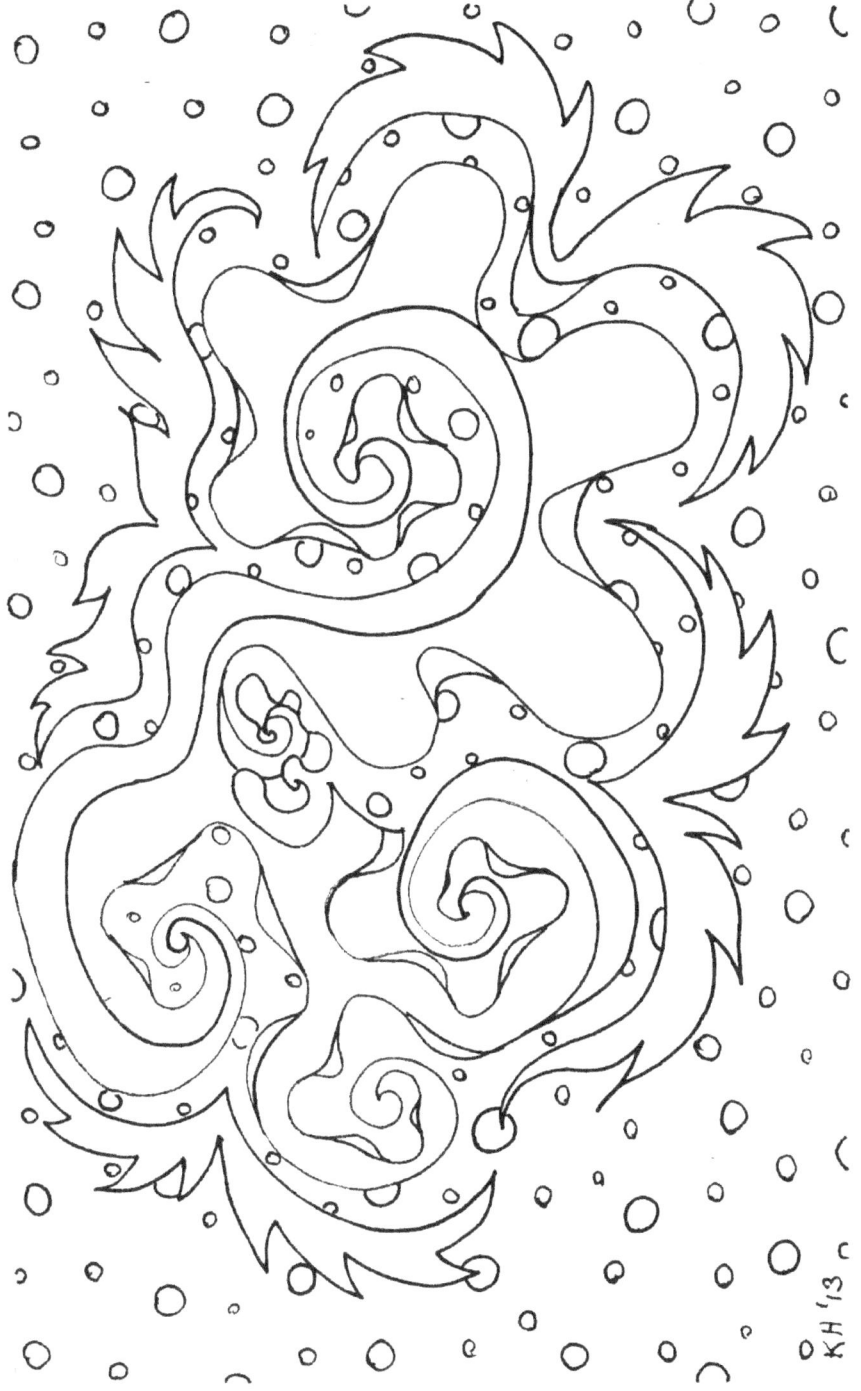

Kathy Carman Henderson

Flowers & Flair

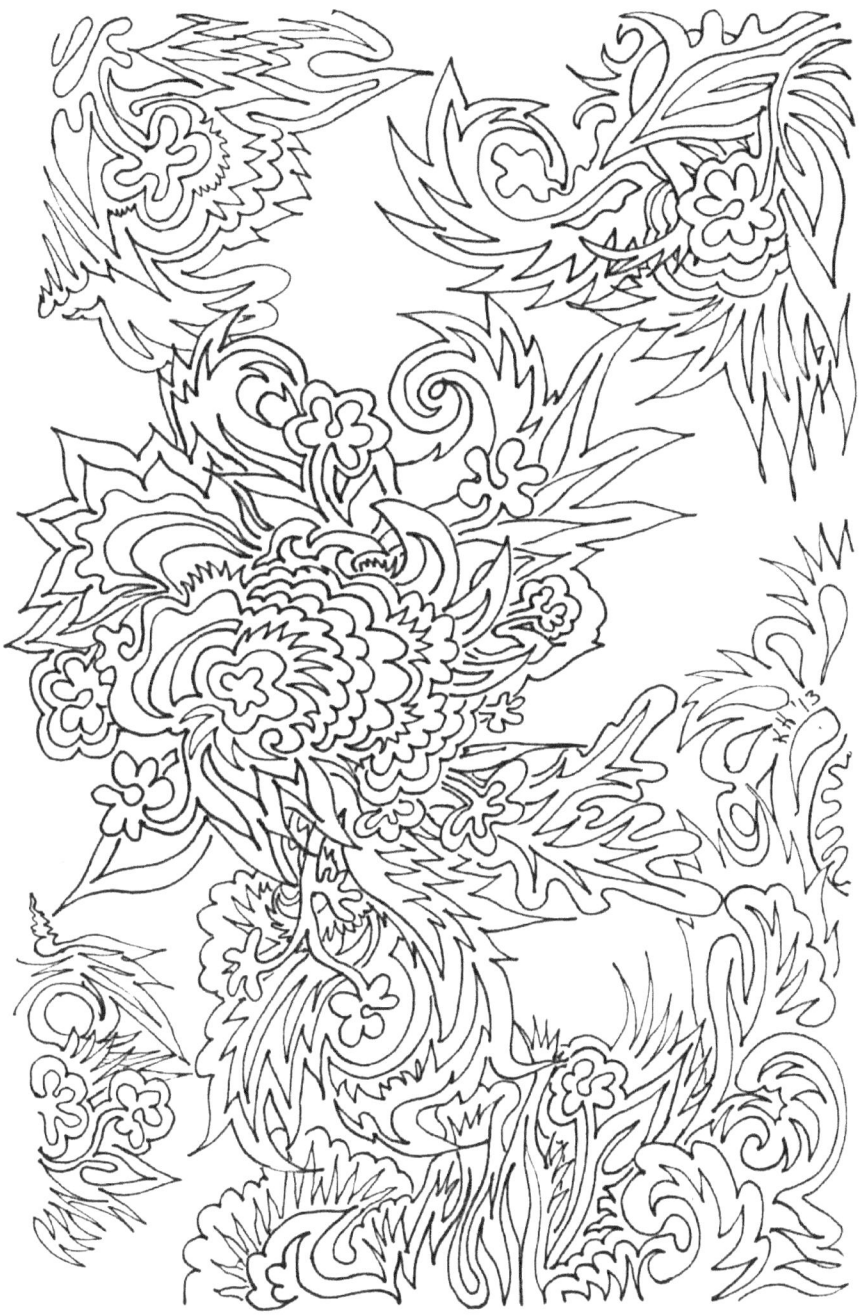

Kathy Carman Henderson

Kathy Carman Henderson is an author, illustrator, and teacher. She started drawing as a young child and continues to find it a valuable part of her life.

Other titles from her include:

Art Coloring Books:
Flow & Flowers

Stories to Learn and Draw by:
The Walking Vegetables
The One You Don't See Coming
The Tiger's Whisker
The Grasshopper and the Ant

Fiction Travel Adventure:
Costa Rican Adventure with Ben and Gretchen

Inspirational:
Party of the Ages

For Future Problem Solving International:
Treffinger, Don. **Tools for Problem Solvers,** (Kathy was a contributing author)

Books illustrated for author Edna Creekmore Carman:
A Day of Rest
Tender Twig

www.ingramcontent.com/pod-product-compliance
Lightning Source LLC
Chambersburg PA
CBHW071754170526
45167CB00003B/1028